THE INTELLECTUAL FOUNDATIONS OF CHRISTIAN AND JEWISH DISCOURSE

The Intellectual Foundations of Christian and Jewish Discourse argues that Judaic and Christian heirs of Scripture adopted, and adapted to their own purposes and tasks, Greek philosophical modes of thought and argument, and explores how the earliest intellectuals of Christianity and Judaism shaped a tradition of articulated conflict and reasoned argument in the search for religious truth that was to be shared through continuing that argument with others.

Professors Neusner and Chilton examine, using the formative sources of Judaism and Christianity, the literary media of adaptation and reform: precisely where and how do we identify in the foundation writings of Christianity and Rabbinic Judaism the new opposing modes of articulated conflict and reasoned argument that through Christianity and Judaism, Greek philosophy and science bequeathed to the West?

This provocative volume provides a unique and controversial analysis of the genesis and evolution of Judaeo-Christian intellectual thought as being informed by the appropriation of Greek philosophy and science and identifies the modes of discourse in the Judaic and Christian intellectual and literary traditions.

Jacob Neusner is Distinguished Research Professor of Religious Studies at the University of South Florida and Professor of Religion at Bard College, New York.

Bruce Chilton is Bernard Idding Bell Professor of Religion at Bard College, New York.

OTHER TITLES AVAILABLE FROM ROUTLEDGE

JUDAISM IN THE NEW TESTAMENT
Practices and Beliefs
Bruce Chilton and Jacob Neusner

THE INTELLECTUAL FOUNDATIONS OF CHRISTIAN AND JEWISH DISCOURSE

The philosophy of religious argument

Jacob Neusner and Bruce Chilton

London and New York

First published 1997
by Routledge
11 New Fetter Lane, London EC4P 4EE

Simultaneously published in the USA and Canada
by Routledge
29 West 35th Street, New York, NY 10001

© 1997 Jacob Neusner and Bruce Chilton

Typeset in Garamond by
M Rules
Printed and bound in Great Britain by
Mackays of Chatham PLC, Chatham, Kent

British Library Cataloguing in Publication Data
A catalogue record for this book is available from the British Library

Library of Congress Cataloging in Publication Data
Neusner, Jacob, 1932–
The intellectual foundations of Christian and Jewish discourse :
the philosophy of religious argument / Jacob Neusner and Bruce
Chilton.
        p.   cm
Includes bibliographical references and index.
1. Talmud—Hermeneutics.   2. Jewish law—Interpretation and construction.
3. Bible. N.T. Epistles of Paul—Criticism, interpretation, etc.   4. Theology—
Methodology—History of doctrines—Early church, ca. 30–600.   5. Midrash—
History and criticism.   6. Dialectic.   7. Reasoning.   8. Judaism—Relations—
Christianity.   9. Christianity and other religions—Judaism.
        I. Chilton, Bruce.   II. Title.
            BM503.7.N478   1997
            296.3'01—dc21   97–3402

ISBN 0–415–15398–0 (hbk)
        0–415–15399–9 (pbk)

CONTENTS

PREFACE

The Egyptians . . . had various beliefs about the way the sky is held up. One idea was that it is supported on posts, another that it is held up by a god, a third that it rests on walls, a fourth that it is a cow or a goddess . . . . But a story-teller recounting any one such myth need pay no attention to other beliefs about the sky, and he would hardly have been troubled by any inconsistency between them. Nor, one may assume, did he feel that his own account was in competition with any other in the sense that it might be more or less correct or have better or worse grounds for its support than some other belief.

When we turn to the early Greek philosophers, there is a fundamental difference. Many of them tackle the same problems and investigate the same natural phenomena [as Egyptian and other sciences], but it is tacitly assumed that the various theories and explanations they propose are directly competing with one another. The urge is towards finding the best explanation, the most adequate theory, and they are then forced to consider the grounds for their ideas, the evidence and arguments in their favor, as well as the weak points in their opponents' theories.

(G. E. R. Lloyd)[1]

In this book we set forth the ways in which, from the very beginning of their work, the Judaic and Christian heirs of the Scripture of ancient Israel made their own Greek philosophical modes of confronting conflict and conducting argument. Our thesis is that at their deepest foundations, Christianity and Rabbinic Judaism take their place wholly within Greek philosophical modes of articulating contradictory propositions and proposing explicit arguments and evidence to show that one is right, the other wrong. In general people understand that these principles of thought form the foundations of

Western knowledge. What we propose to demonstrate is that at the very primary stages in the presentation by both heirs of Israelite Scripture and faith, these same principles of thought governed – because Christian theologians and Judaic sages in the Land of Israel could do their work in no other way.

Along these same lines, many take the quite reasonable view that in one way or another Judaism and Christianity accommodated their Israelite inheritance to the Graeco-Roman intellectual context. But in our view, from the very outset the Israelite heritage was perceived through the intellectual prism of that philosophy. Our argument is that, from their first writings, Paul's letters and the Mishnah, through their climactic statements out of late antiquity, Augustine's *City of God* and the Talmud of Babylonia, Christianity and Judaism undertook their generative and formative thought wholly within, completely at home in, the Greek philosophical milieu, so far as that intellectual world required the explicit articulation of dispute and validation through rigorous argument of one position over the other, contradictory one.

When Judaism and Christianity from their initial writings made their own these Greek philosophical modes of framing propositions and arguing their merits within a shared rationality, the Western Judaic and Christian tradition of science and philosophy was born. And, as we show here, that intellectual appropriation of a mode of thought alien to ancient Israel in its nurture of home-born, revealed truth took place among the very founders of Rabbinic Judaism and Christianity, the sages of the Mishnah, Talmud, and Midrash of Judaism, and the apostle St Paul and the Fathers of the Church of Christianity, respectively. It was wholly within the framework of Greek philosophy that the Judaic sages and Christian theologians learned those lessons concerning the logic that forbade holding contradictory propositions and compelled sound, analytical argument to validate or disprove a fiercely defended position. And, we cannot stress too much, it was at the very beginnings, the point at which both religions were taking shape, that the intellectual revolution represented for the heirs of Israelite Scripture by the appropriation of Greek philosophy and science took place.

So both religions, each fairly claiming continuity with the ancient Israelite heritage, took shape within the effort to effect a remarkable innovation in that heritage. Christian theologians ("saints") and Judaic sages ("our sages of blessed memory") faced a dual task, both intellectual and aesthetic. It was a labor not only of thinking in ways for which Scripture did not prepare them. It also required their substantiating their views in a manner of dialectical argument and analytical demonstration formerly not contemplated at all. The new age of reason required finding a language and aesthetics for expressing in the new modes of thought the distinctive modes of thought and argument that now concerned them – a new way of setting forth the results of a new way of thinking without precedent in the Israelite heritage.

Along the way new modes of thought required new media of expression, so the Fathers of the Church and our sages of blessed memory had to invent new ways of talking about what we now deem new truth. This new truth spoke of God made flesh, on the one side, the whole Torah, oral as well as written, on the other. For the Greeks studied the here and now of nature and society, but the theologians and sages took up issues of the nature of God, on the Christian side, and the meaning of sanctification, on the Judaic. That is why the problem facing Scripture's heirs required not merely a new vocabulary for familiar things, but a new way of thinking about what was, in fact, quite unfamiliar. It was as if for communication of a fresh message they had to adapt, to a quite new set of rules of syntax, a language that had for ages used its own vocabulary and grammar to make its own statements. In the initial contrast portrayed in the opening two chapters between how Jesus and Paul confronted and articulated conflicting opinions, on the one side, and how Scripture, the *Damascus Covenant*, and the *Community Rule* of the Qumran library and the Mishnah lay out laws, on the other, we see the nature of the intellectual challenge that the Fathers of the Church and our sages of blessed memory successfully met.

In ancient Israel the articulated and systematic exchange of conflicting views, together with arguments in favor of the one and opposed to the other, for which the German word, *Auseinandersetzung*, serves best, was unknown. Prophesy, laws with accompanying myths of origin and authority, narrative of exemplary times past, prayer, poetry, and wise aphorisms – these afforded no expression to arguments concerning the truth or falsity of general propositions. Prophesy did not argue but declared truth in God's name. The law invoked its own myth at nearly every clause: "The Lord spoke to Moses saying, speak to the children of Israel and say to them . . . ." The aphorisms of sagacity hung suspended in air, lacking argument and denied the reenforcement of challenge met and overcome. Above all, narrative of times past cobbled together diverse viewpoints and propositions and recorded the result as though in a seamless story. So in Israelite literature prior to the Mishnah of *c.* 200 CE, for Judaism in Hebrew and Aramaic,[2] and the letters of Paul from *c.* 50 CE, for Christianity, we find nothing comparable to Greek philosophical discourse, no analytical inquiry, replete with objection and counter-argument, into conflicting propositions, no sustained and rigorous dialectical arguments such as form the glory of Plato's Aristotle.

Take the case of scriptural narrative, for instance. There, as Professor Lloyd points out for the mythological world of other Mediterranean peoples so in ancient Israel, two or more contrary opinions can stand side by side without a trace of acknowledgement that both cannot be true. To give one obvious example, Gen. 1:1–2:3 and 2:4ff. set forth two different, and necessarily conflicting stories of creation; the same narrative accommodates two stories of Noah, and many other points of conflict, without a trace of explicit recognition that the stories present incompatible theories on their stated topics. Possibly excluding the book of Job, we cannot find any counterpart in the Hebrew Scriptures of ancient Israel ("the Old Testament") to the reasoned construction of contradictory propositions in the form of articulated disputes and debates that proves quite commonplace in the ancient world and would characterize Judaic writings from the Mishnah forward.

Now, on the basis of Israelite Scriptures' tolerance of contradictory accounts of the same facts, advances in learning and even reasoned exchanges of propositions, argument, and evidence with a view to persuading the other that one is right, prove impossible. If Noah took the animals two by two, he cannot have taken them in lots of seven – and so forth. By contrast, Greek science and philosophy educated the West in the view that conflicting opinions should be examined and tested so that the true one could be distinguished from the false one. But before the first century for Christianity represented by Paul, and for Judaism represented by earliest groups of the sages of the Mishnah, debating propositions were recognized to conflict, and doing so through systematic and reasoned argument appealing to canons of evidence and rationality shared by those who held contradictory views, made no appearance whatsoever. Wherever we turn among the Hebrew- and Aramaic-language writings of Israelites, whether in the Apocrypha and Pseudepigrapha of the Hebrew Scriptures or among the library found at the Dead Sea, we see people imitating Scriptural modes of thought and expression.

That meant either ignoring or dismissing views contrary to one's own, which, often as not, were also represented as God's. The

Synoptics represent Jesus' conflict with the Pharisees in such a way that the Pharisees, straw men, held no positions worthy of serious analysis and argument. But Paul's letters formed systematic and reasoned arguments with real people, holding their views on solid grounds. The library at Qumran contains no articulated disputes in which both parties share premises and differ on details, arguing about the differences. But the Mishnah is built out of disputes and debates among people with sufficient convictions in common to engage in reasoned argument. The break would take place in the letters of Paul and his successors, on the one side, and in the Mishnah and that document's continuators, on the other.

Then and only then, for the joint heirs of Israelite Scripture do we find the presentation of two conflicting views and efforts at the formation of arguments to validate one of them over the other. Disputes and debates from that point forward fill the pages of Christian and Judaic holy books. For their part Christian theologians, defining themselves against Judaism, even composed systematic writings taking up propositions they imputed to Judaism and showing the evidence and arguments out of a commonly-affirmed Scripture that sustained the Christian and refuted the (supposed) Judaic position. On the basis of the systematic presentation of disputes and debates in the writings of Judaic sages and Christian theologians, therefore, we identify that initial generation in the formation of Christianity and Rabbinic Judaism as the starting point of the Western Christian and Judaic appropriation – adoption and adaptation for the sacred sciences – of the Greek philosophical discovery that opposites must confront and reason must resolve the confrontation. At the foundations of all logical inquiry lay the philosophers' insistence that conflicting principles cannot both be right, and merely announcing an opinion without considering alternatives and proposing to falsify them does not suffice for intellectual endeavor. And with the recognition of that possibility, not only identifying conflict in opinion but taking up reasonable argument for one side and against another side of a mooted point, Greek philosophy engaged in debate, for integral to the articulation of differing views is analytical testing of contradictory propositions. What was true of science pertained to civilization in all aspects:

In their very different spheres of activity, the philosopher Thales and the law-giver Solon may be said to have had at least two things in common. First, both disclaimed any supernatural authority for their own ideas, and, secondly, both accepted the principles of free debate and of public access to the information on which a person or an idea should be judged. The essence of the Milesians' contribution was to introduce a new critical spirit into man's attitude to the world of nature, but this should be seen as a counterpart to, and offshoot of, the contemporary development of the practice of free debate and open discussion in the context of politics and law throughout the Greek world.[3]

(G. E. R. Lloyd)

Accordingly, for the first time in the history of humanity, it was with Greek philosophy (inclusive of science) that conflicting propositions were systematically tested with a view to determining which one was right.

Christianity and Judaism framed matters as they did, not because they needed to bridge a perceived gap between the natural sounds of their language and the alien music of the language of those they wished to address. From the Mishnah, Judaism's first canonical document after Scripture, and Paul's letters, Christianity's original statement, the sages and theologians conducted thought in no other way but the philosophical one. That is why they articulated what was subject to dispute and proposed through reasoned argument to distinguish true from false. Not by ignoring contradiction but resolving it, not by merely asserting conviction but demonstrating its ineluctable soundness, they chose solely through the dispute and debate, the dialectical argument and the systematic analytical inquiry, to uncover the very truth of the Torah (for Judaism), the *logos* which is Christ, for Christianity.

So for Judaism as for Christianity, the new modes of thought emerge not as instrumental and contingent but as necessary – and, within the context of truth revealed through Christ the *logos* or through the Torah, also as sufficient. That is why the theology of Christianity and the norm-setting law of Judaism alike (and, as a matter of fact, of Islam) have been to begin with conducted in accord with the rules of rationality set forth by Greek philosophy. Conflict between principles is recognized, reasoned argument in behalf of the one and against the other is set forth, decisions are reached within the concordant conviction that opposites conflict, and conflict must be resolved through reasoned argument, relevant evidence, and rational inquiry.

But how did the philosophical and scientific method take over modes of thought and inquiry characteristic of Judaism and Christianity as these have flourished in the West? Since, as we said, it was not by reason of Scripture (which provided its heirs in nascent Christianity and formative Rabbinic Judaism no models, either literary or intellectual) to deal with the powerful intellectual instruments of dispute, debate, and dialectical argument, it was through the formation of a new way of writing down the results of a new way of thinking. It follows that what we wish to trace in this book is this: *How did the earliest intellectuals of Christianity and Judaism shape and give voice and form to a tradition of articulated conflict and reasoned argument in the search for religious truth that was to be shared through reasoned argument with others?*

What we do not know is where the theologians and sages learned to think like philosophers; all we know is that they did. Ours is not an account of cultural history, origins and borrowing and influences and contacts. From the way in which people set forth their thought we work our way back to how they thought, why they presented their ideas in one way, rather than in another, and what rationality dictated for them the natural way of thinking. So we center our interest on the written evidence of processes of thought that have come to full exposure in completed writings. We focus especially on the solid evidence afforded in literary media of adaptation and reform. Precisely where and how do we identify in the foundation-writings of Christianity and Rabbinic Judaism the new modes of articulated conflict on the one side, and the new media of reasoned argument on the other, which through Christianity and Judaism (and Islam) Greek philosophy and science would hand on to the West?

The answer to that question we set forth through specific writings that reveal the beginnings, under Christian and Judaic auspices, of the modes of thought and reasoned expression characteristic of Western philosophy and science. What is at stake is clear: since it was under those Christian and Judaic (and later on, Islamic) auspices that Western philosophy and science have been conducted until very nearly our own time, here, in these particular writings, we propose to identify the bridge between what is critical for the West in Greek philosophy and what is formative for the West in the canonical, intellectual heritage formed by Christianity and Judaism. For in late antiquity both great traditions determined to set forth not only revealed, but reasoned, truth, and both formulated powerful arguments such that would compel others to concede the claims of the faithful. Each was intellectually ambitious and wished to play its part in the world of rationality constituted by Graeco-Roman antiquity.

We demonstrate here that both certainly did succeed in finding modes of articulating conflict in such a way as to compel assent from all reasonable, right-thinking people. That is why we claim that in the kinds of writings we set forth we find the origins of Western rationality – if also its intolerance of error; the beginnings of reasoned dispute about truth accessible to all equally – and also the start of that intellectual self-confidence for which, alas, many have paid a grievous price. Specifically, what we show here is that when we reach the later first and second century, we find in the joint heirs of Scripture an unprecedented interest in articulating argument and confronting conflict in the quest for a single, compelling truth. Writings of the later centuries of late antiquity would then make the next move, from explicitly-formulated conflicting propositions to systematic, rule-governed arguments – dialectical arguments – meant to analyze the conflict and uncover the truth.

In the classical Judaic sources we find disputes about a shared agendum, in which two or more positions are stated side by side and tested with the view of determining, or demonstrating, that one was sound, the other not. In Christianity, theologians from Paul forward were prepared to set forth reasoned propositions and sustain them with well-composed arguments, all in accord with the prevailing expectations of informed intellectuals. Mere assertion, on the one side, or simple appeal to revelation, on the other, ceased to suffice in the intellectual life of the nascent religious systems. If, to take one example from Chapter 1, we set side by side a legal passage of the Dead Sea Scrolls with a passage on the same theme in the Mishnah, we see that the former alleges facts, the latter is studded with vivid disputes on the character of rules. The one asserts, the other demonstrates. So, too, when we contrast Jesus' arguments with his critics with those of Paul, as in Chapter 2, we see the difference between assertion and polemic on the one side, and, on the other, the effort to compose an argument capable of persuading those not in agreement from the beginning.

Accordingly, the plan of the book is simple. We set forth a synthetic picture of matters, preliminary generalizations for further study, rather than complete description of the texts with an analysis of every piece of evidence.[4] In alternating chapters, formative sources of Judaism (Chapters 1, 3, 5, 7) and Christianity (Chapters 2, 4, 6, 8) yield their evidence to sustain our hypothetical propositions concerning philosophy (Chapters 1–4) and science (Chapters 5–8) that (1) both nascent Rabbinic Judaism and early Christianity recognized and articulated conflicting propositions; (2) both taught themselves how to conduct dialectical arguments in resolving the conflict; (3) both formed arguments out of the data of natural history; and (4) both appealed to arguments based on the regularity and order of the social world of history. These four simple propositions bear the burden of the book. In laying out the main lines of the matter, we anticipate further study will carry forward nuance and modification at every detail. But the main points sketched out here we think will stand.

They concern the fundamental structure of thought. Important questions of history and context elude all answers. So all we undertake here is to set forth the evidence for the thesis announced at the outset: integral to Judaism and Christianity from the very beginning is the recognition of conflict of opposed view and respect for reasoned argument for one and against another of two conflicting positions. Urgent questions of historical interest on the one side, and motivation on the other, find no answer here. For instance, as stated, we do not know where theologians and sages learned the lessons that govern their thought and expression. Concerning their education and social background we possess remarkably limited information and, in the case of the framers of the Rabbinic literature, none that passes the usual tests of historical criticism.

While we see the canonical writings of nascent Christianity and formative Judaism as marking a complete turning away from the received Israelite heritage, we also do not speculate on the motivation for the theologians' and sages' break with all prior Israelite writing, which both parties cite lavishly but – in intellectual terms of modes of thought and argument – imitate not at all. Before Christianity, within the world of ancient Israel in the Hebrew and Aramaic languages, no one wrote letters such as Paul's, and before the Mishnah no prior law code attempted anything remotely comparable to it. Here we portray, as a sharp break with their intellectual roots, both Rabbinic Judaism and nascent Christianity, but we cannot account for that break, except with the claim that the way writing portrays the course of thought tells us how the writers conducted thought; we know no way to break out of that circularity. We are left to affirm, for good and sufficient reasons, that the theologians and sages could accomplish their goals only in the way that they did – by rejecting the entire Israelite heritage of writing and thinking – but we cannot explain why they adopted such intellectually disruptive goals and not ones in harmony with that heritage.

It is for a different reason from the absence of sources or the failure of our own imagination that we also do not raise questions of authority. These questions concern how the theologians and sages formulate appeals beyond articulated and compelling reason, to God or Scripture for instance. That is because we plan a separate, also comparative study of Scriptural and other sources of authority in nascent Christianity and formative Judaism. Here the evidence abounds, but we have to learn how to address it.

Both authors gladly acknowledge a debt to Mr Richard Stoneman at Routledge, whose guidance in the planning of this book required us to set forth a brief, sharp statement, rather than the rather elaborate, but therefore less accessible, one we had originally contemplated. We are always free to expand and extend matters. But at the outset a clear and simple statement serves best.

Responding to our consultation, the great Cambridge Classicist, G. E. R. Lloyd, whose works have so deeply influenced ours over the years, raised questions that served to clarify our thesis and focus it more sharply. We appreciate his generosity in sharing his judgment and sharp insight.

To President Leon Botstein and the academic administration of Bard College both authors are indebted for the long-term opportunity to work together. This and a number of other books began in our shared teaching during the autumn semester each year, made possible by Bard's appointment of Mr Neusner as Professor of Religion at Bard under terms compatible with his position at the University of South Florida.

Mr Neusner also expresses his thanks to the University of South Florida, where he holds tenure as Distinguished Research Professor of Religious Studies, for a generous Research Fund and, more important, for the terms of appointment that create an ideal situation for teaching and scholarship.

Mr Chilton extends his special appreciation to the congregation of the Church of St John the Evangelist, which has permitted him the latitude for which the Anglican Church is justly famous.

Jacob Neusner
University of South Florida and Bard College
and
Bruce Chilton
Bard College

PART I

CONFRONTING CONFLICT

Articulating Disagreement in a Reasoned Setting

1

CONFRONTING CONFLICT IN THE MISHNAH

[A] Honeycombs: from what point do they become susceptible to uncleanness in the status of liquid?

[B] The House of Shammai say, "When one smokes out [the bees from the combs, so that one can potentially get at the honey; before that point the honey, that is, the liquid, is inaccessible and therefore inert]."

[C] The House of Hillel say, "When one will [actually] have broken up [the honeycombs to remove the honey, for only at that point is the honey really accessible as liquid and therefore an active component]."

(Mishnah-Tractate Uqsin 3:11)

So the Mishnah draws to a close, at the end of sixty-two tedious tractates of law on as many topics, broken up into more than five hundred and fifty chapters comprised of equally picayune and recondite rulings. The highly formalized character of the composition – topic sentence, followed by two carefully balanced rulings, each bearing an attribution to an authority – competes for attention with the peculiarity of the subject-matter. Here is how the sages of the Mishnah articulate both established principles and secondary disputes about them, the Mishnah's characteristic mode of setting forth its laws and conflicts concerning them.

Before we take up the substance of the dispute, let us tackle the simpler question of its rather odd form. To make sense of the formulation of the dispute before us we look in vain for help in Scripture which provides no precedent for this austere presentation of the law, and disputes concerning the law. Formally, Scripture presents rules in quite a different manner. For one thing, Scripture attributes laws to God via Moses. Consequently, no one (except a rebel or a heretic) disagrees about principles or details. The Mishnah, for its part,

3

presents undisputed laws anonymously but its massive corpus of disputes are presented only in the names of specific, historical authorities. More striking still, Scripture embeds the laws in a rich mythic narrative. Of a story of origins, in time or beyond, the Mishnah's framers know nothing; their document takes no specific place for itself; it opens without identifying its audience, concludes without demanding assent or even drawing out general observations, for example about justice or sanctification. Scripture's laws articulate their purpose, for instance, "Thus you shall keep the people of Israel separate from their uncleanness, lest they die in their uncleanness by defiling my tabernacle that is in their midst" (Lev. 15:31), and Scripture's laws also set forth not only details of rules but governing principles, for instance, "You shall not hate your brother in your heart but you shall reason with your neighbor . . . you shall not take vengeance . . . but you shall love your neighbor as yourself. I am the Lord" (Lev. 19:17–18). The Mishnah concludes with that same laconic mode of speech, lacking all specific focus, to whom it may concern, with which it begins: talking to no one in particular about nothing of very compelling interest in the workaday world.

If, as Rabbinic Judaism would claim, the Mishnah stands in a chain of tradition with God's revelation of the Torah to Moses at Sinai, so that Shammai and Hillel are portrayed in Mishnah-tractate Abot, the Fathers, as receiving "Torah" from masters who served as disciples to masters backward to Joshua to Moses to God, the composition offers remarkably little grounds to validate that claim. Nothing in Scripture prepares us for the form of the law – an articulated conflict – let alone its substance, a purity-ruling out of all phase with Lev. 11–15 and its counterparts on the same general topic. And yet, a brief inspection will show us that the passage, like numerous others,[1] addresses an issue that Aristotle takes up and that occupies philosophy from his time to ours, namely, the relationship of what is potential to what is actual.

By the measure of its peculiarity within the Israelite context, the substance of the dispute matches the form. What is at stake in this rather odd dispute would hardly engage a prophet or exegete of Scripture, let alone a philosopher in that or any other time, but only a nit-picking priest intending to preserve cultic cleanness in order to carry out his duties in the Jerusalem Temple.[2] At issue is the status, as to cultic uncleanness or cleanness, of a liquid that is susceptible to the uncleanness deriving from sources of uncleanness specified by Lev. 11–15. The premise of the question, "from what point does liquid

CONFLICT IN THE MISHNAH

become susceptible," is that liquid may or may not be susceptible to
uncleanness at all. The question rests on the premise set forth by the
Mishnah's reading of Lev. 11:34, 37, which specifies that food that
has been wet down is susceptible to the uncleanness imparted by
various specified sources, but food that has remained dry is insusceptible. Specifically, Mishnah-tractate Makhshirin holds that when food
has become wet because of deliberate action, then we take its condition into account. But if water has accidentally or unintentionally
come upon the food, we do not take its condition into account.
Hence, intentionality governs, a conception of which, in this context,
Scripture knows nothing. With these two principles in mind, we
turn to the dispute represented by the little composition before us.

Since an intelligible, consequential dispute can take place only
within a shared consensus – people who do not speak the same language may engage in conflict but cannot conduct an argument – we
begin by asking what principle or rule both parties share. From the
answers to the question we derive the point in common. One party
maintains that the liquid of honeycombs is susceptible to uncleanness
when one has smoked out the bees, the other, when one has broken
the honeycombs. Clearly, therefore, when I have access to the honey,
so that I may make use of it, the honey is susceptible. It follows, furthermore, that liquid which is not accessible to human use (in this
context) is deemed insusceptible; Lev. 11:34, 37 are read to make that
point. So the articulated dispute concerns the point at which honey
becomes susceptible to uncleanness, and the two positions specify a
sequence of occasions: (1) the bees are smoked out or, later, (2) the
honeycombs actually are broken and the liquid flows. The dispute
underscores the shared premise, which, as I said, is that of Mishnah-
tractate Makhshirin in regard to Lev. 11:34, 37. So the articulation of
the dispute underscores the shared principle and appears to yield a
refinement of no very considerable interest, and none to anyone who
does not observe the rules of cultic cleanness set forth in the book of
Leviticus.

But what is the principle at hand? Surely, readers must even now
have dismissed as rubbish any allegation that great principles of
Western philosophy find replication in any way, shape or form in the
Mishnah, its method and its message. But a second look should lead
us to discern otherwise. For I have interpolated some words to make
clear that in context inheres the issue of whether what is potential is
treated as though it were now actual and real. That is to say, do I take
account of what potentially may happen? Or do I treat as fact only

5

what has happened? The specifics of the case make sense only if we see the case as exemplary of the issue of how the potential relates to the actual (egg and the chicken, the foetus to the child, the acorn to the oak would serve equally well).

The House of Shammai – supposedly a legal circle of the first century CE – say that once you have smoked out the bees, you have access to the honey. What is potential is treated as equivalent to what is actual. Since you can get at the honey, the honey can be useful to you and so is susceptible. The House of Hillel – the matched opposite, generally thought to derive from the same period[3] – say that only when you have actually broken the honeycombs by a concrete deed is the honey susceptible. What is potential is not taken into account, only what is actual.

So at stake in this odd passage is a very familiar debate. It specifically concerns how we sort out issues involving the potential and the actual. Do we treat what is going to happen as a fact defining our ruling on what has happened? Or do we deem what is going to happen as null until it has actually taken place? The oak inheres in the acorn, which then causes the oak to come into being. Or change and circumstance may intervene, so that the acorn may never become the oak at all, and these issues too must enter our decision. If we wished to sort out issues of causation and teleology involving what is potential and what is actual, a variety of cases would serve equally well.

The one at hand would scarcely take first place among the candidates for inclusion in a class lecture on the potential and the actual. The case itself requires altogether too generous a volume of explanation. It hardly touches on the everyday, though it surely takes shape around the here-and-now of bees, honey, and honeycombs. We need not speculate on what motivated the writers to lay out matters as they have, but we must recognize that integral to their program is the articulation of a dispute. As we shall note in due course, the framers cannot have accomplished their goal without making reference to named disputants, who both moot a detail and share and confirm a principle.

Clearly we are in the hands of a very odd author, who mounts discourse at three dimensions all at once: (1) through *how* things are said, with the form of the dispute a highly formalized mode of discourse, as we shall note in due course, (2) through *what* is said, and (3) through *what lies beneath the surface* of things as well. That author has enormous respect for us, the readers, assuming that we read and hear with so astute and sentient an interiority as to gain the message even in the subtle media through which it is conveyed. I can identify hundreds of compositions and even whole composites in which the Mishnah's framers work out in acute detail their speculation on the matter of actuality and potentiality, which is an issue characteristic, in particular, of Aristotle within the larger theory of causation. In presenting our proposition, we have followed the manner of the Mishnah, moving from the acutely concrete onward to broader abstraction. Now let us proceed to the main point.

It is simple: the articulated confrontation with conflict in the writings of groups portraying themselves as that "Israel" of which Scripture spoke, first takes place in the Mishnah, a document set forth as a law code but in fact framed so as to address also a set of issues of a largely philosophical character. No prior Israelite writing finds urgent the presentation of conflicting positions on a common case, none seeks through such an articulation of disputes over minor points the confirmation that beneath conflict is a shared and established principle. Occupied with questions that in its context characterized philosophical inquiry such as being and becoming, the genus and the species, the nature of mixtures, types of causation with special attention to intentionality, above all the hierarchical classification of all manner of things, the Mishnah carries on discourse at two levels. On the surface, homely problems concerning rules and regulations predominate. But a second look time and again shows how these problems embody in concrete terms the same controverted questions that philosophy takes up in abstract ones. And a third inspection turns up the Mishnah's power through its deft formulation of rules to set forth generalizations, principles rich in qualifications on the one side, implications for quite different cases on the other.

More to the point, the purpose of the presentation, time and again, aims at articulating two sides of a single question. That is the point of special interest here, namely, where the explicit confrontation with conflicting principles or viewpoints enters in. If the aesthetic glory of the Mishnah is its capacity to speak, like a poet, in humble language about sublime truths, in tangible images about what is ineffable, the dynamic power of the Mishnah flows from its systematic formulation not of propositions but choices inhering in propositions. The laws then present not only information – do this, do that – but issues subject to conflict. They generate intellectual energy only because they are laid out to formulate principled positions in conflict with other, intersecting ones. The framing of the compositions aims at establishing the given, then raising the problem, much as a composition for

Euclid's geometry begins with the axiom and proceeds to the theorem to be demonstrated (or refuted). So, too, the document does not set out to prove one position and disprove another, but rather to show how competing answers to the same questions may play themselves out. The Mishnah imposes on those who would study it the discipline of attentive reading, which finds its reward in the intellectual challenges of conflict over matters of high abstraction and heavy weight. When we examine other Israelite counterpart law codes, the comparison will yield an account of an active, as against an inert, presentation of law. With so much taking place inside the representation of the law in the Mishnah, no wonder its framers did not find necessary any kind of mythic setting for their work.

The disputes then impart huge energy to the document. For that purpose the Mishnah requires named figures to represent the points in dispute, much as the great philosophical writers would create names to stand for viewpoints in dialogue. Nearly every composition of the Mishnah encompasses disputed points, which are articulated so that two contradictory positions are presented, and to such a presentation named authorities prove absolutely necessary. Without the named sages the document loses its dynamism.

The disputes serve yet another purpose, signalling where we stand, in an unpunctuated (and memorized) text, in the unfolding of a given topical presentation. For a close inspection shows that the formulation of the composition as a whole – a series of undisputed rules – aims at identifying at the end such a disputed point. A sequence of uncontested rules will commonly reach its conclusion and climax at the one debated point, and only with the uncontested rules in mind do we understand what is at issue in the dispute. And while subject to dispute may be a fine point of law, inherent in the dispute will be buried conflict on a common principle, so that the named authorities who are party to the dispute will stand for the two possible positions on the conflicted principle. Hence what looks at first glance to constitute little more than a niggling detail will emerge as the point and purpose of a large-scale composition.

The upshot for this account of how, in earliest Rabbinic Judaism, people confronted conflict is simple. The document's framers can accomplish their goals, as the document reveals those goals, only by articulating and confronting conflict, and, for that purpose, it was also necessary to identify parties to the conflict and formulate for the parties systematic and coherent positions. These positions then would guide their holders in determining how to rule in concrete cases, and when the sum of the concrete cases is taken, the generative principles represented by them all will readily emerge. If, then, in Plato's dialogues, a name stands for a viewpoint to be set forth and argued out in the setting of a debate with a contrary viewpoint identified with a name, the Mishnah deserves comparison with those dialogues. And the one really striking difference is that while Plato's Socrates asks what, exactly, is justice, our sages of blessed memory occupy themselves with conflict over who owns a cloak that two persons claim, or how to adjudicate possession of a sliver of land or the carcass of a gored cow.

From the Mishnah forward Rabbinic Judaism would take as its hallmark respect for dispute and enormous esteem for a well-crafted argument. But looking backward, we realize that the document marked a drastic break from the entire Israelite past. For neither formally nor (in our context) substantively does the Mishnah bear comparison with any prior compilation of rules, but only contrast with them all. Certainly the framers found ample guidance for their work, for the making of law codes, whether those of Exodus or Leviticus or Deuteronomy, or those of Elephantine and Qumran, formed a genre of Israelite writing. But the Mishnah's writers rejected every available model.

On the other side, whatever those other codes, whether Scriptural or extra-Scriptural, bear in common, none remotely compares with the Mishnah. All the post-Pentateuchal codes take up topics of the Pentateuchal laws, and so do the Mishnah's framers. But among them, only the Mishnah frames an agendum of its own, one as ambitious and wide-ranging as the Deuteronomic laws (Deut. 12–26), the glory of the Pentateuchal compilations. But – more to the point – what both formally and intellectually sets the Mishnah apart from all Israelite law codes, the provision of disputes on points of law, on the one hand, and the names of authorities that are party to those disputes, on the other, proves remarkable. No Israelite writing before the Mishnah followed the formal procedures of the document in setting forth conflicting positions on a common agendum and naming the authorities who espoused the respective views. But then none, before the Mishnah (and its continuators in the two Talmuds), aimed at transforming law into jurisprudence, and jurisprudence into philosophy.

To make these general remarks of comparison and contrast more concrete, let us turn back and conduct a comparison between prior law codes and the Mishnah. What we shall see is that, in a general way, a post-Pentateuchal and Pentateuchal law code stand sufficiently close together for meaningful comparison, but both differ, and differ in the same ways, from the Mishnah so that comparison and contrast prove parlous indeed. We begin with a code fairly close in time to the Mishnah, two writings of laws preserved in the library at Qumran. Some time toward the end of the second century BCE an authority whose writings would be preserved in the library at Qumran set forth the rule governing the Israelite community gathered in a covenant around a particular teacher and determined to live together in accord with laws particular to that group.

The Community Rule, as set forth by Geza Vermes,[4] covered three topics: entry into the covenant and the community doctrines, statues on the council of the community, and rules addressed to the master. While the very basis for the community's existence found definition in confrontation with the rest of Israel and the world beyond, the Community Rule is set forth without a single named authority on the one side, and without the presentation of disputed propositions and arguments for or against them, on the other. So the children of light, like the children of Israel of the Pentateuch, received instruction from the master, but the children of darkness, like the followers of Korach, are acknowledged only by curses and dismissed to outer darkness.

Among the topics covered by the Community Rule, a list of penalties for infractions of the law captures our attention, because we find a counterpart treatment of the same general problem in the Mishnah, and comparing the two pieces of writing about the same subject allows us a clear entry into the important traits that distinguish the Mishnah:

> If any man has uttered the [Most] Venerable Name even though frivolously or as a result of shock or for any other reason whatever, while reading the Book or praying, he shall be dismissed and shall return to the Council of the Community no more. . . .
>
> Whoever has deliberately lied shall do penance for six months.
>
> Whoever has deliberately insulted his companion unjustly shall do penance for one year and shall be excluded.
>
> Whoever has deliberately deceived his companion by word or by deed shall do penance for six months.[5]

It suffices to note that the rule is given anonymously; no disputes are recorded, and no contrary propositions or opinions are given a hearing.

So too, in the same library, the so-called Damascus Rule sets forth a series of laws, which, formally, do not present jarring differences from the laconic statements above. A composition on the Sabbath, for instance, yields the following:

> No man shall work on the sixth day from the moment when the sun's orb is distant by its own fulness from the gate. . . . No man shall speak any vain or idle word on the Sabbath day. He shall make no loan to his companion. He shall make no decision in matters of money and gain. He shall say nothing about work or labor to be done on the morrow.[6]

For a model of how to set forth rules about this and that, perhaps topically related, perhaps not, the authors in both cases can have found guidance at Deut. 12–26, with its long sequence of miscellaneous rules about this and that:

> A woman shall not wear anything that pertains to a man, nor shall a man put on a woman's garment. . . .
> If you chance to come upon a bird's nest in any tree or on the ground, with young ones or eggs and the mother sitting upon the young or upon the eggs, you shall not take the mother with the young.
> When you guild a new house, you shall make a parapet for your roof. . . .
> You shall not sow your vineyard with two kinds of seed.
> You shall make yourself tassels on the four corners of your cloak.[7]

Now it suffices to make the point that, in the Mishnah, a new and unprecedented mode for the presentation of law has taken shape, to cite a comparable composition. What we shall see, in the intersecting rule governing making plans on the Sabbath for secular matters, is a different mode of discourse altogether:

> [A] A man should not hire workers on the Sabbath.
> [B] And a man should not ask his fellow to hire workers for him.
> [C] They do not wait at twilight at the Sabbath limit to hire workers, or to bring in produce.
> [D] But one may wait at the Sabbath limit at twilight to guard [produce, and after nightfall] he brings back the produce in his hand.
> [E] A governing principle did Abba Saul state, "Whatever I have the right to say [to another person to do], on that account I have the right to wait at twilight at the Sabbath limit."
> (Mishnah-tractate Shabbat 23:3)

The first thing we notice is an interest in refinement and qualification, which yields not only the rule of [A]-[B], but, in their contrast, a general principle, subject to application in a wide variety of circumstances, namely, what one may not do on his own, he also may not ask his neighbor to do. [C]-[D] likewise present a rule and its qualification, once more yielding a principle subject to generalization. But the most striking entry is at [E], where a named authority makes his contribution, which is a proposition joining the point of [A]-[B] and [C]-[D] into a moral rule: what I may do, I may ask another to do, but what is illicit for me I cannot send an agent to do in my behalf. Clearly, we find ourselves in a very different world from that set forth in Deut. and carried on in the law codes preserved in the Qumran library.

The remarkable, indeed unprecedented character of that world emerges when we move forward in the comparison by seeing how Scripture and the Mishnah deal with exactly the same problem, namely, determining the requirements of justice in a conflict over property. Scripture's narrative mode of presenting and solving the problem, and that of the Mishnah, do not conflict but the way in which Scripture sets forth the problem and its solution and that of the Mishnah scarcely intersect:

[A] Two lay hold of a cloak –

[B] this one says, "I found it!" –

[C] and that one says, "I found it!" –

[D] this one says, "It's all mine!" –

[E] and that one says, "It's all mine!" –

[F] this one takes an oath that he possesses no less a share of it than half,

[G] and that one takes an oath that he possesses no less a share of it than half,

[H] and they divide it up.

[I] This one says, "It's all mine!" –

[J] and that one says, "Half of it is mine!"

[K] the one who says, "It's all mine!" takes an oath that he possesses no less of a share of it than three parts,

[L] and the one who says, "Half of it is mine!," takes an oath that he possesses no less a share of it than a fourth part.

[M] This one then takes three shares, and that one takes the fourth.

(Mishnah-tractate Baba Mesia 1:1)

[A] Two were riding on a beast,

[B] or one was riding and one was leading it –

[C] this one says, "It's all mine!" –

[D] and that one says, "It's all mine!" –

[E] this one takes an oath that he possesses no less a share of it than half,

[F] and that one takes an oath that he possesses no less a share of it than half.

[G] And they divide it.

[H] But when they concede [that they found it together] or have witnesses to prove it, they divide [the beast's value] without taking an oath.

(Mishnah-tractate Baba Mesia 1:2)

The point of the Mishnah-paragraphs is that, where there are equally valid claims, we split the object that is at issue equally between the claimants. The Mishnah-passage presents three exemplary cases, all of them following the same formal pattern and adhering to the same rules of syntax. Our author thinks we are very careful readers (or listeners), who will put together the main point he wishes to make by seeing the patterns of not only language but thought. Just as he has so formulated his ideas in language as to make it easy for us to memorize what he says, so he has laid matters out in such a way that we, for our part, can see the main point that his three cases mean to make. What are some of the generalizations that the passage yields?

1 In a case of conflict over right of ownership of an object, where the claims are of equal merit, we impose an oath on each party to assure that he or she is telling the truth, and then divide the object equally. That is, obviously, because each party claims the whole of the object. Then there is no choice but to give half to each.

2 The same principle – adjudicating the conflicting claims, once confirmed through an oath, by giving each party half of the part that he or she has claimed to own. If one alleges he owns the whole, and the other only half, then the second party has conceded the claim of the first to the other half. At issue then is only ownership of the second half, and that we divide, hence the first party gets three, the second, one share of the whole.

3 The third case repeats the first. What it adds is only a procedural matter, H.

Then can we say that a single generalization covers the entire triplet? Of course we can: *where there are equally valid claims, we split the object that is at issue equally between the claimants.*

Does our author tell us that? No and yes. He gives us no generalization at all. But he assumes that we will see what the three cases have in common and recognize that that is the governing principle. Focusing upon his cases – the extent of the claim to the object, whole (1:1) or part (1:2), whether or not an oath is necessary to validate one's claim (1:3) – our author has made his main point by indirection. Yet he knows we will not miss it, and, of course, no one can. Now, as a matter of fact, the oral Torah goes over a problem that the written Torah sets forth in its own way as well.

In fact the Mishnah has given us an abstract representation of concrete events, which we might render as "if two lay hold of a cloak," "if this one says . . .," "if that one says," "then this one takes, and that one takes, and they divide . . .," and so on throughout. The omission of the "if," and the presentation of the whole in very brief clauses serve very well to give us what looks like a concrete case, a kind of event, but is in fact a general rule, yielding in the repeated statements of that rule an abstract generalization. Can a writer in the Israelite world say "where there are equally valid claims, we split the object that is at issue equally between the claimants" in some other way than this? The following shows us a different way of making the same statement:

> Then two harlots came to the king and stood before him. The one woman said, "Oh, my lord, this woman and I dwell in the same house; and I gave birth to a child while she was in the house. Then on the third day after I was delivered, this woman also gave birth, and we were alone; there was no one else with us in the house. Only we two were in the house. And this woman's son died in the night, because she lay on it. And she arose at midnight and took my son from beside me, while your maidservant slept, and laid it in my bosom. When I rose in the morning to nurse my child, behold, it was dead; but when I looked at it closely in the morning, behold, it was not the child that I had borne."
>
> But the other woman said, "No, the living child is mine, and the dead child is yours.":
>
> The first said, "No, the dead child is yours, and the living child is mine."
>
> Thus they spoke before the king.
>
> Then the king said, "The one says, 'This is my son that is alive, and your son is dead,' and the other says, 'No, but your son is dead, and my son is the living one.'"
>
> And the king said, "Bring me a sword."

So a sword was brought before the king. And the king said, "Divide the living child in two and give half to the one and half to the other."

Then the woman whose son was alive said to the king, because her heart yearned for her son, "Oh, my lord, give her the living child and by no means slay it."

But the other said, "It shall be neither mine nor yours; divide it."

Then the king answered and said, "Give the living child to the first woman and by no means slay it; she is its mother."

And all Israel heard of the judgment which the king had rendered, and they stood in awe of the king, because they perceived that the wisdom of God was in him, to render justice.

(1 Kings 3:16–28)[8]

Does this passage make the same point as our Mishnah-paragraph? Indeed it does, for there is strict justice: where there are equally valid claims, we split the object that is at issue equally between the claimants. Will the author of our Mishnah-paragraph have found the principle expressed in this story surprising? So far as the rule of law is concerned, the answer of course is negative. But the point of the story before us, and the purpose of the Mishnah-paragraph at hand, are quite different. Each author has chosen to make his own point, and he has done so, as a matter of fact, by finding a medium of expression that matches his purpose.

The Mishnah's writer wants to speak of principle and procedure: when is an oath required, when not? That is his main point. We know it, because it comes at the end; it is startling; there is no preparation for it; and it marks the climax and conclusion of the piece of writing at hand. When the same thing is said three times, and then something else is tacked on, our attention is drawn to that new matter. When, then, we look back and see see how, in the prior writing, the oath has been introduced as integral, we realize what has happened. What will be the main point is introduced quite tangentially and repeated as a given; then we assume that given is not at issue. But at the end, we are told that what we took for granted is in fact not routine. An oath is required only if there is a conflict, but if each party concedes the other's claim, or if there are witnesses to establish the facts, then no oath is at issue at all. What was entirely tangential now turns up as the main point. The framer of the passage has made it certain we would be jarred and that our attention would be drawn to that surprising, and we now realize, critical issue.

That our narrator in the story of Solomon and the two widows has chosen a medium suitable for his message hardly requires specification. He sets the stage in the opening paragraph: the one party states her claim, the other the opposing claim. The rule of law is clear: split the difference. The issue of procedure is of no consequence to our narrator, so he does not say that each party must prove her claim, for example, taking an oath (or whatever procedure pertained at that point in Israel's history). The king then makes his elaborate preparation to carry out the rule of law. The woman who spoke first speaks again, then the other speaks as briefly as before. The king repeats the language of the first woman: "by no means slay it," now adding, "she is its mother." Is the point of the story the law that where there are equally valid claims, we split the object that is at issue equally between the claimants? Hardly! The point of the story is at the end: "And all Israel heard of the judgment which the king had rendered and stood in awe of the king because they perceived that the wisdom of God was in him, to render justice." The form of the story bears that message, as much as the contents articulate it. And, it is clear, any other form but narrative will not have accomplished the storyteller's purpose.

We see how cases of the same kind can be used for entirely different ends, and, when an author proposes to set forth his purpose, he chooses language and syntax and forms of communication that serve that purpose. The author of the story about Solomon wants to say that Solomon had divine wisdom; the case makes that point by showing how Solomon transcended the limits of the law through not (mere) mercy but profound understanding of obvious facts of human nature. The author of our Mishnah-paragraph is talking about different things to different people, and his choices show the difference. He gives us not narrative, which serves no purpose of his, but brief and artful clauses, each free-floating, all of them joining together to create cases. He then finds for himself laconic and detached language, not the colorful and evocative phrases used by the other. Contrast the understatement with the overstatement, the one casual, the other rich in heightened and intense language:

[C] this one says, "It's all mine!" –
[D] and that one says, "It's all mine!" –

"Oh, my lord, this woman and I dwell in the same house; and I gave birth to a child while she was in the house. Then on the third day after I was delivered, this woman also gave birth, and we were alone; there was no one else with us in the house. Only we two were in the house. And this woman's son died in the night, because she lay on it. And she arose at midnight and took my son from beside me, while your maidservant slept, and laid it in my bosom. When I rose in the morning to nurse my child, behold, it was dead; but when I looked at it closely in the morning, behold, it was not the child that I had borne."

But the other woman said, "No, the living child is mine, and the dead child is yours.":

The first said, "No, the dead child is yours, and the living child is mine."

Contrast, again, the undramatic resolution with the tension and the resolution of the tension that form the centerpiece of the narrative:

[F] **this one takes an oath that he possesses no less a share of it than half,**

[G] **and that one takes an oath that he possesses no less a share of it than half,**

[H] **and they divide it up.**

And the king said, "Bring me a sword."

So a sword was brought before the king. And the king said, "Divide the living child in two and give half to the one and half to the other."

Then the woman whose son was alive said to the king, because her heart yearned for her son, "Oh, my lord, give her the living child and by no means slay it."

But the other said, "It shall be neither mine nor yours; divide it."

Then the king answered and said, "Give the living child to the first woman and by no means slay it; she is its mother."

It is difficult to imagine two more different ways of saying more or less the same thing. The Mishnah's author speaks in brief clauses; he uses no adjectives; he requires mainly verbs. He has no actors, no "they did thus and so." He speaks only of actions people take in the established situation. No one says anything, as against, "the king said . . . ." There is only the rule, no decision to be made for the case in particular. There is no response to the rule, no appeal to feeling. Indeed, the Mishnah's author knows nothing of emotions, Scripture tells us "because her heart yearned," and the Mishnah's author knows nothing of the particularity of cases, while to the Scripture's narrator, that is the center of matters. The Mishnah presents rules, Scripture, exceptions; the Mishnah speaks of the social order, Scripture, special cases; the Mishnah addresses all Israel, and its principal player – the community at large – is never identified. Scripture tells us about the individual, embodied in the divinely-chosen monarch, and relates the story of Israel through the details of his reign.

When we remember that the author of our Mishnah-passage revered Scripture and knew full well the passage before us, we realize how independent-minded a writer he is. On the surface he does not even allude to Scripture's (famous) case; he does not find it necessary to copy its mode of presenting principles. And yet what differentiates the main point, "they divide it up" and "divide the living child in two"? (And who requires "and give half to the one and half to the other"!)" Only these words make a material difference: *the living child.* Since our author knew Scripture, he had to have known precisely what he was doing: the affect, upon hearers or readers of his rule, of the utilization of the precise ruling of Solomon.

All that changes is "living child" into "cloak." Everything is different, but everything is also the same: the law remains precisely what the narrator of the tale about Solomon knew, as a matter of fact, it to be. Then the law is not the main point, either of Scripture's tale, or of the Mishnah's rule. The Torah – God's revelation to Israel – lives in the details, and through our two authors, both of them immortal for what they wrote and perfectly capable of speaking to minds and hearts of ages they could not have imagined, God speaks through the details.

The substantive shifts match the formal ones. The change from anonymous, free-flowing narrative to the introduction of articulated differences in rulings assigned to named authorities and the utilization of rigidly formalized rhetoric of the Mishnah prove as striking. When we compare the passage of the Mishnah just now examined with the one with which we commenced, we note one important difference. Our opening composition sets forth a dispute, following the use of highly formalized rules of construction – statement of the issue, X says, Y says. Not only so, but the exact wording assigned to the one party matches, even in number of syllables in the Hebrew, that assigned to the other. Once more, the case of Mishnah-tractate Uqsin suffices to show the careful formal balance:

the House of Shammai say, mi/she/ye/har/her
the House of Hillel say, mi/she/ye/ra/seq

The dispute-form, indicative of the Mishnah and amplified in the

Gemara, finds no counterpart in any earlier writing in Israel. In all of the Hebrew Scriptures, for example, with their rich record of conflicting viewpoint we have nothing like a public dispute, a debate comprising balanced, reasonable arguments (prophets, for instance, do not debate with kings or priests, and only Moses debates with God, and then not on equal terms). Not only so, but while more than a single opinion may register in a given context, one opinion is never juxtaposed with some other and set out with arguments on behalf of the superiority of one position over another, or one explanation over another, for the purposes of a reasoned exchange of opinion and argument. That is to say, Elijah and the priests of Baal do not enjoy equal time to explain why fire consumed Elijah's, but not the priests', offerings.

The singularity of the dispute-form proves still more striking when we once more call to mind the genre of Israelite literature to which the Mishnah most obviously may be alleged to correspond, law codes.[9] The manner in which laws are set forth in Exodus (JE), the Holiness Code (P), Deuteronomy, let alone the library at Qumran and in the Elephantine papyri, for example, in no way proves congruent with the manner in which the Mishnah sets forth laws. To take two striking differences already adumbrated, the former attributes nothing to named authorities, the latter names authorities in nearly every composition; further, the former never contains articulated debates on laws but only apodictic laws; the latter is made up of explicit disputes of rulings on a shared agendum of issues. A third difference, from Scripture's codes in particular, is to be noted: the absence of a myth of authority, corresponding to "The Lord spoke to Moses saying, speak to the children of Israel and say to them." To take an obvious point of comparison, set side by side, the Mishnah's presentation of Sabbath law and that in the Dead Sea library bear few points of formal comparability at all, as we have already noticed.

True, the Mishnah's law refers constantly to the substance of Scripture, even though citations of Scriptural texts prove rare and at best episodic. That makes all the more remarkable the persistence of disputes as the norm, unattributed, normative law as the mere background for the setting forth of vivid contentious discourse. It is equally true that the Mishnah's law intersects with the law portrayed in prior collections, which is hardly surprising given the reference-point of all collections in Scripture. That again underscores the significant point: while in some details, the snippets of laws preserved at Qumran intersect in contents with bits of the laws of the Mishnah and related writings, in form we find only differences.[10] It is the striking fact, therefore, that the first piece of writing in the history of Judaic religious systems to set forth a program of debate is the Mishnah.[11] Elsewhere, differing opinions prove abundant. But occasions in which differing opinions are set forth in the form, and for the purpose, of debate prove few indeed.[12]

The upshot is that the Mishnah, from start to finish, forms a vast arena for debate. And, as Lloyd points out, beyond the recognition that "natural phenomena are not the products of random or arbitrary influences but regular and governed by determinable sequences of cause and effect,"[13] it is articulated dispute precipitating fully spelled-out debate that forms the distinguishing mark of Greek science and philosophy, and it is with the Mishnah that debate entered the public discourse of the Judaism put forth by our sages of blessed memory. In the Mishnah's representation of matters, the sages always "knew and criticized one another's ideas," just as did the early Greek philosophers. And, in the context of prior Israelite writing, they find no antecedents or models or precedents for their insistence upon debate, (implicit) face-to-face exchange of contradictory views, with provision for sorting out difference through reasoned exchange.[14]

If the presentation of disputes distinguishes the Mishnah from all prior Israelite law codes, it is the formulation of debates to amplify what is subject to dispute that demands philosophy's attention. For here what is implicit in the dispute is made accessible. Not only so, but the logic that dictates the course of legal thought finds explicit presentation much as, in the dispute-form, the point of conflict and its subterranean principle come to expression. The disputes of the Mishnah do not always spill over into fully-spelled-out debates, but, in one way or another, attentive disciples may readily construct debates from what disputes contain. Hence a complete account of how, in Rabbinic Judaism, sages in a philosophical manner confronted conflict and articulated issues of a philosophical character must include a brief encounter with the expansion of a dispute into a debate.[15] While the Mishnah contains its share of debates, the Tosefta, a compendium of compositions that complement the Mishnah, presents us with a striking case of how a dispute is amplified. In the present case, the debate concerns the governing analogy, and the principle that we settle a case by finding the appropriate analogy to an already-settled case is introduced in an explicit manner.

What we see is how argument by analogy and contrast works to sort out issues subject to dispute.[16] The case concerns the disposition of what is subject to doubt – along with mixtures, a favorite theme of

the framers of the Mishnah. The principle of debate is simple: introduce an analogy to the case at hand and show that in the analogous
case, your ruling, not the contrary one, governs. The required reply is,
show that that analogy is inexact and therefore null, but a different
analogy governs, which favors the opposite conclusion. Hence we
confront an exercise in employing arguments by analogy, with the
task of refining the bases for comparison and contrast. In the following case, what we do not know is the status of objects immersed in an
immersion-pool that, at a given point in time, are found to be lacking in the requisite volume of water and so unable to effect the
purification of what is immersed. Specifically, how do we dispose of
those objects immersed in the time from the last point at which it was
known that the pool had a valid volume of water?

[A] "An immersion-pool which was measured and found lacking –
all the acts requiring cleanness which were carried out depend-
ing upon it

[B] whether this immersion-pool is in the private domain, or
whether this immersion-pool is in the public domain –
[Supply:] objects that have been immersed are unclean.]

[C] R. Simeon says, 'In the private domain, it is unclean. In the
public domain, it is clean.'"

Thus far we have the statement of the case. Now comes the dispute
and debate:

[D] Said R. Simeon, "There was the case of the water-reservoir of
Disqus in Yabneh was measured and found lacking."

[E] "And R. Tarfon did declare clean, and R. Aqiba unclean."

[F] "Said R. Tarfon, 'Since this immersion-pool is in the assumption of being clean, it remains perpetually in this presumption
of cleanness until it will be known for sure that it is made
unclean.'"

[G] "Said R. Aqiba, 'Since this immersion-pool is in the assumption of being unclean, it perpetually remains in the
presumption of uncleanness until it will be known for sure
that it is clean.'"

The principle is, do we focus upon the prevailing assumption as to
the status of the pool, and confirm that status, or do we declare the
governing analogy to be the status of the unclean object that was
immersed in the pool, and confirm that status? The former status is
confirmed as valid, since we have assumed the pool was valid until we

discovered that it was lacking in the requisite volume of valid water; the latter status is confirmed as unclean, since we assume objects that have been declared unclean remain so until they are validly purified. Now at stake is, which is the governing analogy?

[H] "Said R. Tarfon, 'To what is the matter to be likened? To one who was standing and offering [a sacrifice] at the altar, and it became known that he is a son of a divorcee or the son of a woman who has undergone the rite of removing the shoe,

[I] for his service is valid.'"

[J] "Said R. Aqiba, 'To what is the matter to be likened?'"

[K] "'To one who was standing and offering [a sacrifice] at the altar, and it became known that he is disqualified by reason of a blemish –

[L] for his service is invalid.'"

Thus far we have the conflict between relevant analogies. Now how is the argument articulated? It is through the challenge of each party to the pertinence of the analogy introduced by the other:

[M] "Said R. Tarfon to him, 'You draw an analogy to one who is blemished. I draw an analogy to the son of a divorcee or to the son of a woman who has undergone the rite of removing the shoe [and is invalid for marriage into the priesthood].

[N] Let us now see to what the matter is appropriately likened.

[O] If it is analogous to a blemished priest, let us learn the law from the case of the blemished priest. If it is analogous to the son of a divorcee or to the son of a woman who has undergone the rite of removing the shoe, let us learn the law from the case of the son of the divorcee or the son of a woman who has undergone the rite of removing the shoe.'"

In fact, as we shall now see, Tarfon's statement of the issue of which analogy governs proves to set matters up to allow Aqiba to settle the question. He does so by differentiating the analogical cases, showing where the true point of similarity – now, he insists, not mere similarity but identity! – is to be located:

[P] "R. Aqiba says, 'The unfitness affecting an immersion-pool affects the immersion-pool itself, and the unfit aspect of the blemished priest affects the blemished priest himself.

[Q] But let not the case of the son of a divorcee or the son of a woman who has undergone the rite of removing the shoe prove the matter, for his matter of unfitness depends upon others.

[R] A ritual pool's unfitness [depends] on one only, and the unfitness af a blemished priest [depends] on an individual only, but let not the son of a divorcee or the son of a woman who has undergone the rite of removing the shoe prove the matter, for the unfitness of this one depends upon ancestry.

[S] They took a vote concerning the case and declared it unclean.'"

[T] "Said R. Tarfon to R. Aqiba, 'He who departs from you is like one who perishes.'"

(Tosefta Miqvaot 1:16–19)

Aqiba finds no difficulty in acknowledging the similarity, but he criticizes the use of the analogy by differentiating, in the manner of Socrates, between similarity and identity. He is able to differentiate ("divide") the analogy into its operative components, and, in doing so, he shows that the analogy as he proposes to apply it sustains his position.

Hearing the language, "Let us now see the governing analogy," will have pleased the Classical philosophers. True, sages' debates on differentiating the like into unlike categories will not have challenged the intellect of the philosophers for whom the question was one of practical, not theoretical, interest. But with the details properly explained, they will have fully appreciated the modes of analytical argument before them and will have founded no reason to dismiss them as other than philosophical. Certainly the basic thrust of the public arguments we have examined – to assess the allegation of analogy or identity between two different things – will have won applause from Plato, as Lloyd states:

The idea that the central task of dialectic is to distinguish the essential similarities and again the essential differences between things is a point to which Plato returns again and again. Plato's main interest . . . is in the material problem of which Forms "agree with" or "share in" which others, rather than in the formal question of the relationships of similarity and difference themselves, and although in various passages he does draw attention to such points as the difference between "similarity" and "identity" and to the distinction between the denial of a term and the assertion of its contrary, it is not until Aristotle that we find a full exposition of the relationships of opposition and similarity.[17]

The basic mode of analytical argument we have examined conforms in its principal traits to Lloyd's account.

The really interesting question that remains is one of how philosophy will have valued the logic before us. In so far as Plato distinguished arguments from proofs, deeming analogy an ultimately unreliable guide, he will have deemed our sages' efforts amateurish. Aristotle too will have found fault. In the end he will have wondered at the thin layer of argument accompanying disputes, at the easy, not terribly laborious proofs for one proposition over another than analogy afforded. Perspective on the cases we have examined comes to us from Lloyd's account of the practice of the explicit analogical argument over time. He states:

> First Plato distinguished merely probable arguments from proofs and drew attention to the unreliability of likeness as a whole in the context of dialectic (while continuing . . . to use analogical arguments extensively . . .). Aristotle then classified analogical argument (the paradigm) as a rhetorical, that is, persuasive, mode of argument and analyzed it from the point of view of the syllogism, where he divided this argument into first an inductive and then a deductive step and suggested that the weakness of analogy lies in the fact that the induction is incomplete. The importance of this becomes clear when we reflect that earlier writers had often tended to assume the validity of their analogical arguments without question and sometimes explicitly claimed that a conclusion which had been recommended by an analogy had been demonstrated. . . . After Aristotle's analysis of the paradigm there was . . . little excuse for later writers to claim that the conclusion of an argument that proceeded direct from a particular case to a particular case had been demonstrated. . . .[18]

The second of the two considerations introduced by Lloyd, the explicit analogical argument that moved from case to case, encompasses the examples given here, and many others like them, in the Mishnah and the Tosefta. It must follow that, in so far as our sages pursued their inquiries through the media of philosophical thought, they took a place well back from the front lines of criticism and reflection. True, philosophy found its place in their reformation of the everyday life of those for whom they set norms. But in so far as the sages turned to analogy and contrast to do their work, measured against the state of the art six centuries earlier, theirs proved a not very advanced exercise of intellect at all. But, as we have seen, in their own context in the name of the oral tradition of Sinai they broke open new paths, in new directions altogether.

The Mishnah marked the first step in the adaptation of philosophical modes of thought to the tasks of Torah-study: the articulated confrontation with conflicting views. The Talmud would set forth the second, necessary step: the formulation of sound analytical tools of inquiry and argument. But if the Mishnah shows us how sages made their own modes of thought in which other, earlier thinkers excelled, the Talmud will give ample evidence of how, in their own right, our sages would make their mark for all time. Where sages would excel is in the formulation of the dialectical argument, and here they developed analytical arguments of remarkable power and originality.

2

CONFRONTING CONFLICT IN THE LETTERS OF PAUL

CONTRADICTION AS AN INTERPRETATIVE PRINCIPLE

Paul is widely and correctly viewed as a revolutionary thinker within Christianity, but the postulates he begins with belong to the bedrock of experience within the movement. In his letter to the Galatians (written around 53 CE), Paul subscribes to the commonly agreed sense of baptism, and goes on to demonstrate that a close connection between baptism and prayer was presupposed:

> When the fullness of time came, God sent forth his son, born from woman, born under law, so that that he might redeem those under law, in order that we might obtain Sonship. And because you are sons, God sent forth the Spirit of his son into our hearts crying, Abba! Father!
>
> (Gal. 4: 4–6)

Contrary to what is sometimes claimed, the Aramaic term "Abba," a direct form of address, would be at home within usages applied to God within sources of Judaism prior to the New Testament.[1] In Paul's understanding, however, it is possible to refer to God as "Abba," although one might be a Greek-speaking Gentile, because in baptism the Spirit of God's own son possesses one's heart. A similar conviction, expressed more fulsomely, appears in Paul's letter to the Romans (8:1–17), which was written some four years after the letter to the Galatians (*c.* 57 CE). Accepting the Spirit of God's son puts one in a fresh relationship to God, and one addresses him in a new way. "Abba" is the word in Aramaic which has best survived multiple translations during the history of the Church, because it has been accepted as the paradigm of how one stands in relation to God through Christ.

To address God as father initially in baptism implies that a

26

continuing and intimate relationship has been established. In fact, in the same chapter of Romans in which Paul refers to Christians' address of God as "Abba," he also explains:

> Similarly, the Spirit also comes to the aid of our weakness; for we do not know just how we should pray, but the Spirit itself intercedes in wordless sighs.
>
> (Rom. 8:26)

That is, a liturgical understanding of prayer is expressly set aside, in favor of an intimate, spontaneous, and even non-verbal conception of prayer. Both baptism and prayer, then, are within primitive Christian experience first of all occasions of Spirit, rather than formalized activities.

Paul's development of an argument on the basis of Scripture in Gal. 4 is inextricably connected with his emphasis upon the activity of the Spirit within those who are baptized. It is vital to recognize that connection before Paul's arguments from Scripture can be understood. The letter to the Galatians is written to a congregation established by Paul, which in his opinion was on the verge of abandoning "the gospel" (Gal. 1:6–10). The fact that Paul opens the letter with that complaint, instead of beginning with his more usual expression of gratitude for the very existence of the congregation concerned,[2] shows how determined he is to insist on what he takes to be a matter of fundamental principle.

The first two chapters of Galatians establish Paul's own apostolic authority within his understanding of the gospel, and he then proceeds to the heart of his argument:

> Stupid Galatians! Who bewitched you, before whose eyes Jesus Christ was portrayed crucified? I want to know only this from you: did you receive the Spirit from works of law, or from hearing with faith? Are you so stupid? Having started with Spirit, do you now finish with flesh?
>
> (Gal. 3:1–3)

The antithesis between Spirit and flesh is basic to Paul's position, and to his experience. He has just argued, in Chapter 2, that no observation of food laws should be permitted to divide congregations in their eucharistic fellowship. That, indeed, is what is distinctive about Pauline practice. While James and Peter and Barnabas accepted that Jewish followers of Jesus and non-Jewish followers of Jesus could pursue their own customs, Paul insisted that Christ supplanted the force of all such customs.

That is the particular context of Paul's famous teaching of justification by faith, which he articulates clearly in Galatians for the first time in his correspondence:

> For I through the law am dead to the law, that I might live in God. I have been crucified with Christ; I live, and yet not I, since Christ lives in me. As I now live in flesh, I live in the faith of the son of God, who loved me and gave himself for me. I do not refuse the grace of God; for if righteousness were through law, then Christ died for nothing.
>
> (Gal. 2:19–21)

Here is the very center of what has been called the mysticism of Paul: the conviction that identifying oneself with Christ in his crucifixion enables one to participate in the power of his resurrection. That becomes the sole principle of Pauline ethics.

When Paul goes on to call his readers stupid, in the passage cited from the beginning of Chapter 3, he is pursuing the same thought in a fierce key of rhetoric *ad hominem*. But he still refers to the portrayal of Jesus' crucifixion as the occasion of their receiving Spirit (Gal. 3:1–3). That is also a part of Paul's mysticism. Baptism is precisely when, for Paul, one is identified with Christ and made a recipient of Spirit.

This emphasis on the reception of the Spirit is Paul's inheritance from Peter, the primary source of his understanding of the gospel he defends (see Gal. 1:15–20). The Petrine insistence upon the inclusion of non-Jews by baptism by virtue of their reception of the Spirit is evident in such stories as Peter's visit to the house of Cornelius (Acts 10), which becomes a precedent cited in the discussion of the place of non-Jews within the movement (see Acts 11 and 15). Paul can cite the support of Peter in his ministry among non-Jews (so Gal. 2:6–10) precisely because Paul represents the extension of a Petrine principle that the Spirit of God defines a new and widened scope of acceptability before God.

Where Paul differs from Peter is in his radically consistent application of the principle of inclusion by means of the Spirit. The Spirit defines Israel in a completely new way:

> For neither circumcision obtains, nor uncircumcision, but a new creation. And as many as walk by this standard, peace upon them and mercy, even upon the Israel of God.
>
> (Gal. 6:15–16)

Paul does what Peter did not: he redefines what is meant by "Israel" in terms of the Spirit. Spirit, received in baptism, takes the place of circumcision as the marker of what constitutes the people of God.[3] It is for that reason that, unlike Peter, Paul comes to demand that Jewish followers of Jesus, once baptized, consistently abrogate their own rules of purity at meals for the sake of fellowship with non-Jewish followers (so Gal. 2).

Pauline rhetoric casts the issue in terms of whether circumcision can be demanded of non-Jewish followers, in addition to baptism, for inclusion in the movement. There were Christian teachers, described in Acts as Pharisees (Acts 15:5), who made just that demand. But James, Jesus' brother, simply instructed that non-Jewish followers keep certain laws of purity for the sake of acknowledging Moses' authority (so Acts 15:13–21), while Peter was even more lenient (Acts 15:7–11). What really divided Paul from the others was not the practice of circumcision, but Paul's demand that the "Israel" of the "new creation" (Gal. 6:15–16) was to live apart from deeds (or "works") of the law.

In that the fundamental term of reference for Paul is "Israel," his systematic statement may still be described as a form of Judaism. But in that he openly and proudly flouts the accepted social markers of that Israel, he needs to explain his position. More especially, he needs to explain what role the law as written – the Scripture – has if Israel is in fact determined by means of identification with Christ.

The situation of Paul's argument on the basis of Scripture in Galatians is a principal determinate of what he says. Included in that situation, as we have seen, is his axiomatic assertion that the Spirit is released in baptism in an identification with Christ. For that reason, he can – without argument – say that the entire experience is commensurate with the righteousness of the primordial patriarch of Israel: "Just as Abraham believed in God, and it was reckoned to him as righteousness" (3:6). But how is the believer in baptism "just as" (*kathos*) Abraham? Abraham in the book of Genesis is called righteous because he believed God's promise that his progeny was to thrive (see Gen. 15:5–6). What is the connection with belief in Christ at the moment of baptism?

Paul answers that question first by saying that it is faith itself which links Abraham and the believer in the act of belief. Faith makes believers, as he says, "sons of Abraham," and even non-Jews who believe are blessed with the blessing promised to Abraham (Gal. 3:7–9). So Paul's initial claim is that the faith one has in Christ is to be identified with the faith of Abraham: that is why, at the close of the letter, he will claim that faith makes "Israel" as a "new creation" (6:15–16).

The obvious alternative to Paul's claim is that Abraham's example is better followed by pursuing the law. In considering that alternative, Paul makes his first great contribution to the Christian interpretation of Scripture. Paul uses Scripture against itself, to prove that it is not a single, literal authority (Gal. 3:10–11):

As many as are under works of law are under a curse, because it is written, "Cursed be everyone who does not remain in all the things written in the book of the law, to do them" (Deut. 27:26). But it is clear that no one is justified before God by the law, "The righteous one shall live from faith" (Hab. 2:4).

So there are two principles in conflict. One says that you have to do all the law, and another that says you need only to have faith.

The conflict is resolved, according to Paul, by Christ. He himself became a curse, because he was hung on a tree as an executed criminal, an accursed person according to the book of Deuteronomy 21:23:

Christ redeemed us from the curse of the law, becoming a curse on our behalf; because it is written, "Cursed be everyone who hangs upon a tree." So the blessing of Abraham extends to the gentiles in Christ Jesus, and we receive the promise of the Spirit through faith. (Gal. 3:13–14)

So there was a curse, but it is used up by the case of Jesus (so Gal. 3:13). The promise of faith, however, is confirmed by Jesus, so that even non-Jews who believe can share in the promise to Abraham (so Gal. 3:14).

The resolution of the promise of faith to Abraham by belief in Jesus within baptism leaves an open question: the exact place of the law. Paul addresses that question in what follows (Gal. 3:15–18). The promise is compared to a will, which can not be changed once the provisions have been made. The promise to Abraham was made to his "seed": the singular rather than the plural is used in the book of Genesis (13:15; 17:8; 24:7). That seed, Paul asserts, is Christ, the point of the promise which can not be annulled by the intervention of the law some 430 years after Abraham.

Up until this point, then, Paul's assessment of the law has been negative. It is the principle of Scripture which can seem to overrule the promise, but which in fact does not. "What, then, is the law?" (so Gal. 3:19–25) is precisely the question Paul proceeds to answer in more positive terms. His answer is that the law's function is literally pedagogical. As the function of a pedagogue in antiquity was to lead children to school, so the law was intended to keep humanity under its constraint until the promise of belief could be fulfilled by faith. The climax is inevitable, but also resonant:

> For you are all God's sons through faith in Christ Jesus; as many as were baptized into Christ were clothed in Christ. There is no longer Jew and Greek, there is no longer slave and free, there is no longer male and female; you are all one in Christ Jesus. And if you are of Christ, then you are Abraham's seed, heirs according to promise.
>
> (Gal. 3:26–29)

The constraint of the law, because it is provisional, comes to an end in the fulfillment of the promise by means of faith.

Two elements stand out clearly in Paul's Scriptural argument so far. First, the use of Scripture against itself, in order to map a conflicting dialectic within the text, turns out to be a governing concern. In that way, Christ is invoked as the principle and the power which resolves the dialectic, so that faith triumphs over the law. Second (and relatedly), law is held to have a provisional function within a progressive view of human experience, such that promise is the vocation of humanity (instanced in Abraham) and the fulfillment of promise is the destiny of belief (realized by identification with Christ).

Neither of these two elements of interpretation, the dialectical and the progressive, could function apart from the underlying axiom which Paul inherited from the Petrine tradition: that baptism into Christ releases the Spirit of God within the believer. Once that becomes the environment of interpretation, contradiction within Scripture becomes dialectical opportunity. Paul's policy is the reverse of claiming that Scripture always says the same thing in the same way. Instead, he argues that Scripture is at odds with itself, until the faith of Jesus Christ is understood to be the purpose that it is pointing towards. That dialectical perspective leads on naturally to the progressive perspective: human experience is held to reveal that the promise of faith makes every other standard, including the law, of only provisional value.

THE CROSS AS HERMENEUTICAL CENTER

Once Paul has invoked his two principles, he is content to restate his theme, in a resounding repetition of the traditional view of baptism as a moment when the Spirit becomes available (Gal. 4:1–7). That, in turn, leads Paul to reminisce about his personal involvement in that process among the Galatians (Gal. 4:8–20). After that parenthesis, he develops an explicitly argumentative style of exegesis:

> Tell me, you who desire to be under the law, do you not hear the law? It is written that Abraham had two sons, one from the slave and one from the free woman. The one from the slave was begotten according to flesh, and the one from the free woman through promise. These things are meant allegorically. The women are two covenants. One is from Mount Sinai, bearing for slavery; that is Hagar. This Hagar is Mount Sinai in Arabia, and corresponds to Jerusalem now, for she serves as a slave with her children. But the Jerusalem above is free; she is our mother.
>
> (Gal. 4:21–26)

The argument involves what Richard Hays has called a "shocking reversal" of expectations, in that Paul associates Sinai and the Torah with Hagar (and therefore with slavery), rather than with Sarah.[4] As Hays is careful to point out, the apparent ease of the reversal is only possible because Paul "has already framed the categories within which his counter reading will proceed."

The categories involved, however, are deeper and more critical than Hays suggests. He portrays a direct link between Paul's reading of Hagar and Sarah and the community Paul addresses, such that "the meaning of the story is found in the church, and the identify of the church is found in the story."[5] That has become a fashionable way to conceive of the relation between text and the interpretative community: the one reinforces the other by means of an apparently independent authority.[6] Paul's theory is much more dynamic, almost tortured by comparison. For Paul the community is constantly convicted by the text of Scripture, and Scripture is even critical of itself. That is the consequence of his dialectical principles.

Once Scripture is seen as at odds with itself, the Torah given at the moment of liberation from Egypt can itself become a new Hagar, which is just how Paul portrays it. "This Hagar is Mount Sinai in Arabia" (Gal. 4:25). Hays represents the difficulty that direct statement has caused:[7]

The notoriously obscure explanation of Gal. 4:25a ("Now Hagar is Mount Sinai in Arabia"), which has attracted numerous emendations in the textual tradition and countless quizzical comments by critics, is actually nothing other than a puff of rhetorical smoke . . . .

Paul's rhetorical engine is definitely running hot at this point, but it is not in the interests of mere effect. Rather, the dialectical truth of the Spirit, which is not released by means of law but in faith, identifies the Torah given on Sinai as what is past. That mountain is not in the land of promise, but on the Arabian peninsula on the way to inherit the promise.

The dialectical rejection of the Torah and Sinai as bearers of the promise to Abraham is now intensified in the same verse, when Paul goes on to say that this Sinai in Arabia "corresponds to Jerusalem now, for she serves as a slave with her children" (Gal. 4:25b). So Paul, having just used geography to show that Torah does not house the promise, now rejects geography, by saying the Jerusalem you can see is not the Jerusalem you aspire to inherit. As he goes on to say, "But the Jerusalem above is free; she is our mother" (Gal. 4:26). Sarah, then, is neither in Arabia nor Jerusalem, but in the freedom which is coming from heaven. Here, in a compact reading of Scripture, we can see Paul's dialectical principle and Paul's progressive principle working together seamlessly.

The synergy is especially apparent, because Paul does not hesitate to draw the negative conclusion from his principles:

But just as then the one begotten according to flesh persecuted the one begotten according to Spirit, so also now. Yet what does Scripture say? "Cast out the slave with her son, for the son of the slave will not inherit with the son of the free woman." Therefore, brothers, we are not children of the slave, but of the free woman.
(Gal. 4:29–31)

At first, it is not at all clear what Paul means when he seems to refer to Ishmael persecuting Isaac in Genesis. What that Scripture speaks of is personal antagonism between Hagar and Sarah, leading up to Sarah's demand that the slave and her son be expelled (Gen. 21:8–10). In so far as there is persecution, it seems to be the other way around, and strictly an adult affair (see the remainder of Gen. 21). Paul is no literalist. Ishmaelites feature among Israel's traditional enemies (so Ps. 83:6), and that is enough for him. And he sees a correspondence to the current policy of some authorities in Judaism for the persecution of Christians, of which he knows because he himself once persecuted the Church (so Gal. 1:13–14).

That means, however, that Paul's negative conclusion concerning the son of Hagar extends beyond rhetoric, and into practice. Citing Paul's quotation and interpretation of Gen. 21, Neyrey draws just the conclusion many commentators have avoided:

> Besides the ritual of boundary making, Paul indicates a second kind of ritual that is appropriate for dealing with polluting invaders who are discovered to have breached boundaries. They must be identified and expelled.[8]

Just as Paul regards the active persecution of the Church as a threat to its existence, so he insists that the only appropriate response to the slave woman and her son in the midst of the Church is to expel them.

The target of Paul's trenchant remark, however, is not Judaism as such. He does not oppose the maintenance of the Torah by circumcised Jews (even those who also believe in Jesus). His vision is that "all Israel" is to be saved, both those who live by the Torah and those who do not (Rom. 11:26, the climax of an argument started in Chapter 9).[9] For both groups, baptism means that they share the faith of Abraham, by means of a righteousness which the Torah and the Prophets provide witness to, but which they alone can not realize:

> Now apart from law God's righteousness has been revealed, attested by the Law and the Prophets, God's righteousness through the faith of Jesus Christ for all those who believe, for there is no distinction.
>
> (Rom. 3:21–22)

The lucidity of Paul's formulation could not be greater; what can make it difficult to grasp is its radicalism. Law here is a means to the end, as Paul also expressly says, "Christ is the end (*telos*) of the Law for the righteousness of all who believe" (Rom. 10:4).

Understanding Law as instrumental, Paul condemns any attempt to make non-Jews obey the Torah as an example of "Judaizing," the term he uses in Galatians (see Gal. 2:14). Of course, other teachers within the Christian movement during Paul's time in fact countenanced – and sometimes demanded – arrangements in which non-Jewish followers of Jesus deliberately kept the Torah to varying degrees.[10] But because Paul's dialectical method had set the Torah against itself, so as to require the principle of Abrahamic faith to resolve the conflict, he excluded any supplementary keeping of the Torah after baptism. That is the slavery he wished to expel.

The radical cutting edge of Paul's logic was not only intellectual, but emotional. Near the end of Galatians, he reveals his volcanic attachment to his dialectical reading of the Torah:

> You were running well: who stopped you from obeying the truth? The persuasion did not come from the one who called you. A little yeast leavens all the dough. I am persuaded about you, that you will not think in any other way, but he who disturbs you will bear the judgment, whoever he might be. And brothers, if I really continued to preach circumcision, why am I persecuted? Then the scandal of the cross would be emptied. Those who trouble you should castrate themselves!
>
> (Gal. 5:7–12)

The interpretation of this passage has proven difficult, to some extent because Paul's rhetoric is fraught.

Why does he speak of continuing to preach circumcision, if only conditionally? The reason is that "he who disturbs" the Galatians has made out a reasonable case against Paul. Paul permits circumcision to be practiced by Jews who believe in Jesus. (Paul himself will say in a later letter that he is proud to become a Jew among the Jews for tactical reasons; cf. 1 Cor. 9:19–23.) If so, Paul is, in a fashion, preaching circumcision: why would he not permit and even encourage the same practice by the non-Jewish Galatians who turn to Christ? That would enable them to practice the "days and months and times and years" (so Gal. 4:10) of the calendar of Judaism, integrated with the conduct of the Temple which united Israel everywhere within a single practice of sacrifice. Paul bitterly complains about such practices, as well as circumcision. But "he who disturbs" the Galatians is simply a consistent follower of Jesus, who believes that the Torah which promises Christ also regulates behavior within Israel, and he plausibly made the claim that Paul's own permission of circumcision among Jews who were baptized made Paul's views suspect.

Paul's emotional response is not only that. He here insists so clearly on the dialectical nature of his reading of Scripture that the principle cannot be mistaken. The consequence of accepting the Torah as regulative is that: "Then the scandal of the cross would be emptied" (Gal. 5:11). The dialectical tension between faith as promise in distinction to the Torah as requirement of obedience had always been there in Scripture; Paul has already explained this in Chapter 3. But the curse of the Torah was used up in the case of Jesus (so Gal. 3:13): that necessary scandal, the scandal of faith condemned by the law, is precisely what the cross of Christ stands for in Paul's mind. The cross is the metonym for the dialectical resolution of faith versus obedience, such that "the Israel of God" is made up of both the circumcised and the uncircumcised (Gal. 6:15–16). Torah in the regulative sense of law no longer has a necessary function. Indeed, those who accept the law gratuitously miss the centrality of the cross.

The Pauline dialectic explains the extraordinary force of the cross within Christian theology, and the vehemence with which its importance is usually defended. It is not only an event, but the fulcrum of interpretation. To interpret Scripture and experience in the light of the cross is a specific intellectual operation. The interpreter first discovers the tensions implicit, in texts or in situations in life, between the requirements of obedience and the promise of faith. Resolution, accepting the pattern of the cross, involves identifying how the burden of condemnation may be borne in hope. "Let me not boast except in the cross of our Lord Jesus Christ, through which the world was crucified to me and I to the world" (Gal. 6:14).

Just as the cross of Christ means that the Torah uses up its capacity to regulate behavior, because Christ became a curse to the law (Gal. 3:13), so the world loses its capacity to constrain Paul himself. Its capacity to mold Paul's behavior is lost. Paul's interpretative dialectics are volatile, because they are applicable – and are actually applied by Paul – to situations in life, as well as to Scripture.

Paul's emphatic call to expel those who would "Judaize" the Galatians is an example of just such an application. As Neyrey suggests, Paul both establishes a boundary around his Church, and enforces it by the authority to exclude those who accept other boundaries. The terms of reference with which Paul draws his boundary – the faith of Abraham actuated in the case of Jesus – are consciously crafted to present believers as the Israel of God, as Paul explicitly says in Gal. 6:15–16. That means that, for Paul, following Jesus is a matter of Judaism, and true Judaism at that.[11] In that regard, he is explicit:

> For he is not a Jew (*Ioudaios*) who is so in appearance, neither is circumcision in appearance – in flesh, but he who is a Jew (*Ioudaios*) is so in secret, and circumcision of heart is in Spirit, not letter; whose praise is not from men but from God.
>
> (Rom. 2:28–29)

Evidently Paul here parts from that Judaism which understands circumcision as an indispensable requirement, in line with Gen. 17:9–14.

His departure is by no means unique or without precedent within the Judaism of his period. Philo contends against the notion that circumcision may be observed simply in a symbolic sense, along with the keeping of the Sabbath, the festal calendar, and sacrifice (*The Migration of Abraham* 189–93). That is a very interesting list in the present discussion, because Paul complains against the Galatians that, in addition to their willingness to submit to circumcision, they would also observe "days and months and times and years" (Gal. 4:10). Where Philo argues against the laxity of some Jews who would symbolize the Torah away,[12] Paul is contending with non-Jews who might fail to see the promise of the Torah in their zeal to apply it literally.

Paul's stance is therefore unmistakable as involving a form of Judaism within the pluralism of his time. That there was deep and hostile opposition is manifest from his letter to the Galatians as a whole. But the interesting thing about Paul, and about the Judaism of his time, is that the argument was conducted in reference to the appropriate definition of "Israel." The movement which centered on Jesus, even in its Pauline form, had not given up on that fundamental identification of the people of God. Quite the contrary: Paul's Judaism was characterized by an insistence that Abraham was to be understood existentially, as well as historically, so that everyone who was joined with Jesus in baptism was a child of Abraham (Gal. 3:7).

TYPOLOGY

Because the relationship with God through Christ is the end and goal of Scriptural interpretation, the regulative function of the law has been superseded. But supersession is not the same thing as replacement. That is eloquently brought out at the close of the book by Ellen Juhl Christiansen:

From my examination of the Pauline material I have further concluded that when baptism functions primarily as initiation rite it also functions as an ecclesiological boundary mark, where circumcision is reinterpreted theologically so that it no longer has such a function. However, the relation between circumcision and baptism is more complex than one of replacement. For, since Paul never talks about covenant as a relationship humans can enter, he also never characterises baptism as a boundary to the covenant. He never associates circumcision and covenant affirmation, but rather states that "circumcision" is of no particular value. Instead "baptism" functions as a unifying factor, "church," ekklesia, becomes the principal term for corporate belonging, and "covenant" is limited to a vertical relationship with God.[13]

As Christiansen rightly maintains, when Paul refers to Hagar and Sarah, the point is not to speak of replacement, but to the two covenants (4:24) as two opposed principles in antithesis.[14] The resolution of that dialectical tension, as we have seen, potentially puts all humanity within the covenantal promise to Abraham by means of the operation of the Spirit in baptism.

Yet there is a tendency in all of this which is inescapable: Torah is placed in a position ancillary to the fulfillment of the covenantal promise in Christ. The redefinition of the meaning of "covenant" – by means of dialectical interpretation – implies that it refers to all humanity, in so far as belief is possible for any given person. That is the "vertical relationship" with God which Christiansen mentions. Torah is now distinguished from covenant, and is only the point of access by which the covenantal promise is realized in the baptismal event which puts the believer "in Christ," to use the well-known Pauline phrase.[15]

Philo makes it apparent that contemporaneous forms of Judaism represented the Torah in its symbolic, rather than in its regulative, value. But the systemic shift involved in Paul's version of the gospel of Jesus consciously moves the Torah from the center of faith to the vestibule by which faith is entered. That is possible because, as we have seen, Scripture is appropriated and applied dialectically. The resolution of the dialectical tension in the view that the promise has been revealed progressively enables Paul to re-evaluate the Torah. In that re-evaluation, the relegation of Torah to an ancillary position was inevitable.

Other forms of Judaism in the time of Paul effectively reinterpreted the Torah with reference to another systematic principle. For the Pharisees, it was the tradition of the sages; for the Essenes, it was the righteous teacher; for the Sadducees, it was the customary practice of the Temple; for apocalyptists, it was the vision of their seers; for Philo, it was Platonic philosophy. Paul's Christ Jesus does not simply reinterpret the law; he abrogates its regulative function by himself being condemned by the law (so Gal. 3:13).

Because Paul is still speaking of the promise to Abraham fulfilled in Israel, his terms of reference are thoroughly Judaic, and his religious system remains a type of Judaism. But it is a type of Judaism on the way to becoming something else. Paul is not yet in the position of the epistle to the Hebrews, where the Scriptures are effectively replaced by Christ:

> Having spoken in many and various ways to the fathers by the prophets, God at the end of these days spoke to us by a Son, whom he appointed heir of all things, through whom also he made the ages.
>
> (Heb. 1:1–2)

That declaration is part of a comprehensive theology of replacement in Hebrews, in which every major institution of Judaism – Scripture included – is held to have been provisional until the coming of Christ.

In *Judaism in the New Testament*, that was the reason for which we took the epistle to the Hebrews, at the end of the first century, to mark the emergence of Christianity as a system of religion distinct from Judaism:

> The dual revaluation, of Israel and Israel's Scripture, is what permits Hebrews to trace its theology of Christ's replacement of every major institution, every principal term of reference, within the Judaisms of its time. Before Hebrews, there were Christian Judaisms, in which Christ was in various ways conceived of as the key to the promises to Israel. Hebrews' theology proceeds from those earlier theologies, and it remains a Christian Judaism, in the sense that all of its vocabulary of salvation is drawn from the same Scriptures which were axiomatic within the earlier circles.
>
> But the Christian Judaism of Hebrews is also and self-consciously a system of Christianity, because all that is Judaic is held to have been provisional upon the coming of the son, after which point it is no longer meaningful. There is a single center with the theology of Hebrews. It is not Christ with Moses, Christ with Temple, Christ with David, Christ with Abraham, Christ with Scripture, Christ with Israel. In the end, the center is not really even Christ with Melchizedek, because Melchizedek disappears in the glory of his heavenly archetype. Christ is the beginning, middle, and end of theology in Hebrews, just as he is the same yesterday, today, and forever (Hebrews 13:8). Everything else is provisional – and expendable – within the consuming fire which is God (12:29).[16]

Hebrews does not simply represent more of the same sort of claim which Paul made, but the elevation of Paul's dialectical and progressive interpretation of Scripture to a systematic hermeneutics of the whole of human experience.

Although what Hebrews marks is a revolutionary development, the principal tool of its transformation is Paul's method of Scriptural interpretation. In the conception of Hebrews, the Temple on earth was a copy and shadow of the heavenly sanctuary, of which Moses had seen "types."[17] A type (*tupos* in Greek) is an impress, a derived version of a reality (the anti-type). Moses had seen the very throne of God, which was then approximated on earth. That approximation is called the "first covenant" (9:1), but the heavenly sanctuary, into which Christ has entered (9:24), offers us a "new covenant" (9:15) which is the truth which has been palely reflected all along.

Hebrews uses the language of "new covenant" in a way Paul does not, because it marks the systemic departure of Christianity from Judaism. But that language is achieved because typology demands that the figures and terms of reference of the Scriptures should look to their fulfillment in the manifestation of Jesus as God's Son. And the force of typology, which became the usual mode of Christian interpretation during the course of the second century, is a function of just the dynamics Paul articulated: the dialectic principle and the progressive principle.

Paul also permits us to appreciate the link between typology and the hermeneutics of the Spirit in baptism, especially in his first letter to the Corinthians (*c.* 56 CE). He works out a comparison between baptism and the experience of Israel at the exodus, in order to show that the Corinthian congregation now, like the Israelites then, should be careful to abstain from idolatry and attendant errors:

> I do not want you to be ignorant, brothers: our fathers were all under the cloud, and all passed through the sea, and all were baptized into Moses in the cloud and in the sea. And they all ate the same spiritual food, and all drank the same spiritual drink. (For they drank from the spiritual rock that was following, and the rock was Christ.) But God was not pleased with many of them, for they were brought down in the wilderness. These became our examples (*tupoi*), so that we might not be desirous of evil, as they desired. Neither become idolaters, just as some of them were, as it is written, "The people sat down to eat and drink and arose to sport." Neither let us fornicate, just as some of them fornicated,

and in one day twenty-three thousand fell. Neither let us tempt
Christ, just as some of them tempted, and they were destroyed by
serpents. Neither complain, just as some of them complained, and
they were destroyed by the Devastater. All these things happened to
them as examples (*tupikos*), and they were written for our admonition, for us – upon whom the final events of the ages have come.

(1 Cor. 10:1–11)

As C. K. Barrett has pointed out, the sense of the term *type* here is
more as "warning example" than as part of an elaborate scheme of
typology.[18] The formal, theoretical statement of Christ's replacement
of the authority of Scripture is not made here, as it is in Hebrews. On
the other hand, Paul does set up the dialectical tension between
Moses and Christ here, such that "we" who live in the time of the
completed promise represent the goal toward which the progressive
meaning of the Scriptures has been pressing all along.

The simplicity of the scheme Paul proposes in 1 Cor. 10 makes it
all the easier to identify the principles which he deploys, the same
principles he crafted in his letter to the Galatians. As in his earlier
letter, the pivot of any comparison is baptism. Indeed, Paul can make
the comparison between Christ and Moses because he assumes without argument that the exodus relates to baptism, and that the
miraculous food and drink provided to Israel in the wilderness relate
to eucharist. These types find their meaning in the present experience
of the community, not simply in the rehearsal of what happened in
the past.

The ease with which Paul makes his comparisons – between Christ
and Moses, baptism and exodus, eucharist and the miraculous provisions in the wilderness – suggests that by the fifties of the first century,
Christians had already developed the custom of preparing new members for baptism in the period prior to Easter and Passover. That
catechesis, involving as it did constant reference to the Scriptures of
Israel as well as to the traditions concerning Jesus, set up a field of tension between those Scriptures as regulative and the same Scriptures as
witness to the promise fulfilled in Christ. As we have seen, Paul's particular contribution to Christian interpretative practice was to
embrace that tension radically, as setting up the antithesis of law and
promise.

The result of pursuing the dialectic in the case of 1 Cor. 10 is that
the example of Moses is designed, not to demand the keeping of
actual Passover (as in Exod. 12), but to prefigure baptism. Similarly,

the regulative force of the Torah is not an issue here; the ethics of the Torah provides admonition – not prescriptions – against the sort of idolatry, fornication, temptation and complaint which the baptismal community might suffer. The way Paul closes his exposition of the exodus typifies his method as it applies to ethical concerns:

> Temptation has not has not taken you, except in a human way; and God is faithful, who will not let you be tempted beyond what you are able to bear, but will provide with the temptation also a way out, so that you are able to bear it.
>
> (1 Cor. 10:13)

Idolatry, fornication, and complaint, then, instance the range of "temptation," the human tendency to resist the Spirit of God. It is no coincidence that, in all the Synoptic Gospels, Jesus' temptation follows his baptism and his acceptance of the Spirit (see Matt. 3:13–4:11; Mark 1:9–13; Luke 3:21–22; 4:1–13). That is the baptismal paradigm, along with the Scriptures concerning the exodus, which are the "texts" of Paul's dialectical and progressive reading.

Although the point can not detain us here, it is necessary to note that Pauline ethics follow upon just the same hermeneutical principles. The types of idolatry, fornication, and complaint are just that: types of temptation and not literal proscriptions. For that reason, Paul does not conceive of his own ethics (that is, ethics after baptism) as a continuation of the law under another form. As he explains in Romans, his most mature theological work, baptism involves a death to sin and the law, and a rising again with Christ:

> Or are you unaware that, as many of us as were baptized into Christ Jesus were baptized into his death? We were buried with him through baptism, into death, so that just as Christ was raised from the dead through the glory of the Father, so also we might walk in newness of life.
>
> (Rom. 6:3–4)

Just as the Scripture as Torah only leads the way to Christ, so the Scripture as instruction only provides the analogy for the ethics of grace. In neither case is the Scripture as such regulative: it functions both in the past and in the present as a type of the promise which is to be fulfilled.

Once Paul laid the basis of typology, it became the common idiom of Christian interpretation in the midst of the religious and philosophical pluralism of the second century. In that environment, in which adherents of various groups were attracted to Christianity, it was imperative to develop an account of the intellectual integrity of faith, an "apology" in the philosophical sense.

Justin Martyr was the most successful apologist in that sense; he crafted his principal theme on the basis of the Gospel according to John. In 151 BC he addressed his *Apology* to the Emperor himself, Antonius Pius. Such was his confidence that the "true philosophy" represented by Christ, attested in the Hebrew Scriptures, would triumph among the other options available at the time. Justin himself had been trained within some of those traditions, and by his Samaritan birth he could claim to represent something of the wisdom of the east. Somewhere between 162 and 168, however, Justin was martyred in Rome, a victim of the increasing hostility to Christianity under the reign of Marcus Aurelius.[19]

Justin argued that the light of reason in people is put there by God, and is to be equated with the Word of God incarnate in Jesus. His belief in the salvation of people as they actually are is attested by his attachment to millenarianism, the conviction that Christ would return to reign with his saints for a thousand years. That conviction, derived from Rev. 20, was fervently maintained by catholic Christians during the second century, in opposition to the abstract view of salvation which Gnostics preferred.

In strictly religious terms, Christianity did not compete well within the second century. Graeco-Roman preferences were for ancient faiths, and the movement centered on Jesus was incontrovertibly recent. Moreover, it could and often did appear to be subversive of the authority of the Emperor. After all, Christians did not accept the Imperial title of *divi filius* (God's son), and actually applied it to their criminal rabbi. And he was a rabbi who was not a rabbi, because the recognized authorities of Judaism did not accept Christians as among their numbers. For such reasons, the persecution of Christianity had been an established policy of state for nearly a century by the time Justin wrote.

The Christianity which Justin defended, however, was as much a philosophy as it was a religion. His claim was that the light of reason in humanity, which had already been indirectly available, actually became fully manifest in the case of Jesus Christ. Jesus, therefore, was the perfect sage, and Socrates as much as Isaiah was his prophet. In that sense, Christianity was as old as humanity; it was only its open manifestation which was recent.

In order to make out his case, Justin used arguments which had been employed before by Philo of Alexandria, but on behalf of Judaism. Philo also identified the *logos*, the prophetic word articulated in Scripture, as the reason by which God created the world and animates humanity. (Unlike Justin, of course, Philo draws no conclusions about Jesus, his contemporary.) Philo even makes out the historical case that Moses was an influence on Plato, so that the extent to which Greek philosophy illuminates God's wisdom is quite derivative. Justin is actually bolder in his Platonism, in that his argument does not rely on such an historical argument, but on the contention that in Jesus the primordial archetype of humanity and of the world itself, the *logos*, became accessible and knowable in a way that it was not before.

In Justin's thought, therefore, what happened was that underlying principles of typology, as well as the method itself, were turned into a comprehensively philosophical account of Christianity. In his history of biblical interpretation, Robert M. Grant refers to Justin's arguments from Scripture as "typology run riot."[20] He cites a particularly tortured exegesis, in which Justin turns (in his *Dialogue with Trypho, A Jew* 77) to Isa. 8:4, in which it is prophesied that "Before the child knows how to call father or mother, he shall take the power of Damascus and the spoils of Samaria in the presence of the king of Assyria." Against Trypho, Justin insists that the child cannot be Hezekiah, the Jewish king. In a very dense series of interpretations, Justin claims instead that the prophecy refers to the gifts of the magi at the time of Jesus' birth. "The king of Assyria" is Herod the great, so called because of his wickedness. Similarly, "the power of Damascus" refers to the devil, associated with that ancient city, whose sinfulness is compounded by further linking it with the "spoils of Samaria."

Grant's reference to Justin's argument as "nonsense" is understandable, coming as it does from a scholar schooled in modern techniques of exegesis. But the point at issue throughout Justin's work really is not just the Scripture. Justin sets his *Dialogue with Trypho, A Jew* in the period after the revolt under Simon called Bar Kokhba (*Dialogue*, Chapter 1), which lasted between 132 and 135. Thematically, Justin disputes Trypho's conception of the permanent obligation of the law (Chapters 1–47), and sees the purpose of Scriptures in their witness to Christ's divinity (Chapters 48–108), which justifies the acceptance of non-Jews within the Church (Chapters 109–36). Trypho, that is, is portrayed as arguing that the systemic meaning of the Scriptures is the Law, while Justin argues that their systemic meaning is Christ.

Justin describes his own development from Platonism to Christianity as a result of a conversation with an old man. The sage convinced him that the highest good which Platonism can attain, the human soul, should not be confused with God himself, since the soul depends upon God for life (Chapter 6). Knowledge of God depends rather upon the revelation of God's Spirit:

> Long ago, he replied, there lived men more ancient than all the so-called philosophers, men righteous and beloved of God, who spoke by the divine Spirit and foretold things to come, that even now are taking place. These men were called prophets. They alone both saw the truth and proclaimed it to men, without awe or fear of anyone, moved by no desire for glory, but speaking only those things which they saw and heard when filled with the holy Spirit. Their writings are still with us, and whoever will may read them and, if he believes them, gain much knowledge of the beginning and end of things, and all else a philosopher ought to know. For they did not employ logic to prove their statements, seeing they were witnesses to the truth . . . . They glorified the creator of all things, as God and Father, and proclaimed the Christ sent by him as his Son . . . . But pray that, before all else, the gates of light may be opened to you. For not everyone can see or understand these things, but only he to whom God and his Christ have granted wisdom.
>
> (*Dialogue*, chapter 7)

Here is a self-conscious Christianity, which distinguishes itself from Judaism and proclaims itself the true and only adequate philosophy. Justin's account of the truth of the *logos* depends upon two sources of revelation, resonant with one another: the prophetic Scriptures which attest the Spirit and the wise reader who has been inspired by the Spirit.

Justin is quite clear, then, that his concern is not with the immediate reference of Scripture, what we would call its historical meaning. That has also come to be known (rather confusingly) as its literal meaning. We prefer the description of "immediate reference": the meaning of Scripture within the conditions in which it was produced. In his *Dialogue*, Justin portrays Trypho as being limited to the immediate reference of Scripture, enslaved by its specification of laws.

Justin is committed to a typological reading of Scripture, the Christian norm during the second century. The prophets were understood to represent "types" of Christ, impressions on their minds of the heavenly reality, God's own son. Isaac, for example, was taken to be a type of Jesus; where Isaac was nearly offered on Mount Moriah in Gen. 22, Jesus was actually offered on Golgotha. That typology, which Paul had initiated in the first century (Rom. 8:32), became a typical motif during the second century. Trypho, by contrast, is portrayed as becoming lost in the immediate minutiae of the prophetic text. So prevalent was this understanding of Judaism, that by the end of the century, Christian theologians called any limitation to the immediate reference of Scripture (its "literal meaning") the "Jewish sense".

Anyone who is familiar with the development of Judaism from the second century onward will see the irony of this understanding of Judaic interpretation. The second century was just the period in Rabbinic Judaism when Scripture was being interpreted in terms of its eternal meaning, when any limitation to its immediate reference came to be overridden by an appeal to the significance of the eternal Torah. Gen. 22 is a case in point: from the second century, it came to be asserted that Isaac *was* slain on Moriah, that he accepted his fate as a fully grown adult, and that God raised him from the dead. In other words, Isaac was a type in Judaism, as well, but of a different truth: an emblem of a martyr's obedience to the Torah rather than of a prophet's vision of Christ.[21]

So what is presented by Justin as a meeting of minds is actually a missing of minds. Both Justin and Trypho in fact make the immediate reference of Scripture ancillary to its systemic significance. But because Christianity is now committed to the *logos* as its systemic center, and Judaism is now committed to the Torah as its systemic center, the two cannot understand one another. Any objection from one side to the other seems silly: it misses the systemic point. In the absence of any language to discuss systemic relationship, the two sides fall to disputing about which makes better sense of the immediate reference (the "literal meaning") of the texts concerned. What is billed as a dialogue is really a shadow play: learned leaders reinforcing their own positions by arguing over what neither side believes really matters.

The genius of Justin certainly does not reside in his confrontation with Trypho, but in his account of how Christianity works as the discovery of meaning. The recognition of God's Spirit in the text on the basis of God's Spirit within the reader is a classic formulation, an articulate development of Paul's teaching (see 1 Cor. 2). That articulation extends also to Justin's usage of typology as embedded in a dialectical reading of the Scripture (as of human experience) so as to discover its progressive sense in the experience of Spirit.

3

CONDUCTING DIALECTICAL ARGUMENT IN THE TALMUD

Dialectic tests, where philosophy seeks, knowledge.
Aristotle[1]

Because they inherited as their foundation-document a corpus of conflict, a heritage of contending statements of norms and laws, the heirs of the Mishnah, proposing to continue its program, found in dialectics the appropriate medium of expression and thought. That formed the medium of choice for accomplishing their task of confronting contention and resolving disharmony. If the Torah of the Lord was to be perfected, as the Psalmist held, then it was through dialectics that our sages would both demonstrate the perfection of the Mishnah, which by the close of late antiquity they held formed the transcription of the oral Torah of Sinai, and also remove the imperfections of the law that the Torah handed on to Israel.

For Rabbinic Judaism from the beginning stressed not the right ruling alone, but the right ruling attained through right reasoning. And that meant the mode of demonstration and not only the proposition counted: the elegant proof, the imaginative argument, the compelling challenge. Not only so, but questions of authority and Scriptural exegesis loomed large in the definition of right thinking.[2] Heirs of so contentious a tradition as the Mishnah had inaugurated learned with their earliest lessons the uses of rigorous contention. Indeed, characteristically the great sages sought not acquiescence with their views but interesting challenges to them. They deemed consequential not the politics of a decision – the number of concurring rulings one could adduce on behalf of a position in a controverted ruling – but the power of persuasion contained within arguments therefor. In the story that follows, a great sage loses interest in life itself when deprived of a worthy debate-partner:

One day there was a dispute in the school house [on the following matter]: As to a sword, knife, dagger, spear, hand-saw, and scythe – at what point in making them do they become susceptible to

47

rich in dynamism, and lavish in intellectual energy. Lazy minds, dull intellects – these found no place in the Talmud, and the document is rich in instances of ridicule or outright expulsion of stupidity.

What, exactly, do we mean by a dialectical argument? Let us begin with an account of dialectics as defined by Aristotle and by Classical philosophy more generally, then turn to cases that set forth the Talmud's version of the same mode of argument. As we shall see, the classification of a certain type of Talmudic argument as dialectical in the conventional sense will prove entirely appropriate. Robin Smith provides the following:

> Generally speaking, the practice of arguing with others on the basis of their own opinions and securing premises by asking questions may be described as 'dialectical argument. . . . I would propose . . . as a definition of dialectical argument in its most general sense, *argument directed at another person which proceeds by asking questions.*[4]

Certain, very specific, types of Talmudic arguments readily conform to that definition, though not all Talmudic arguments qualify as dialectical.[5] Now Smith elaborates on this matter in the following language:

> The word "dialectical" comes from a verb, *dialegesthai*, which means, "argue." Arguments are verbal disputes in which each party attacks and defends positions, arguments can be won and lost. Here we already have an important distinction from demonstrations, in which attack and defense play no part. Dialectical argument differs from demonstrative reasoning in that it is intrinsically a kind of exchange between participants acting in some way as opponents. . . . Socrates took his philosophical mission in life to be a kind of testing or examining of the beliefs of others through questioning. . . . The majority of [Plato's] written works take the form of dialogues in which Socrates questions various interlocutors. These depictions of dialectical exchanges are more than a device of presentation for Plato; he gives the name "dialectic" to the method of philosophy itself. . . . [Dialectical argument] differs from demonstration, which must deduce from first principles and not from what people think. . . .[6]

Finally, let us ask what a dialectical method should allow us to accomplish. In Smith's terms, it is:

> to make us able to deduce the conclusion we want from premises

conceded by the opponent we are faced with. That can be accomplished if we can find premises that have two properties: [1] the desired conclusion follows from them, and [2] the answerer will concede them. . . .[7]

Now let us turn to the specific case of the Talmud's dialectical, or moving, arguments.

What, exactly, do we mean by a "moving argument"? It is one that transcends the juxtaposition of propositions, arguments, and evidence, that lifts up the argument out of its original, propositional context, and imparts to the argument dimensions vastly exceeding the initial frame of reference: from cases to principles, from law to jurisprudence, from thesis to antithesis to synthesis, in terms used only much later on but appropriate within the Talmud's own framework. This labor of elevating the argument from its initial setting the Talmud carries out by treating propositions, arguments, and evidence to a process of interchange and challenge, composing out of the pronouncement of differences of opinion an ongoing, unfolding argument, one in which one point is countered by another, so that, what then follows is not a recapitulation of what has been said, but an interchange of reason and argument. Then because the players listen thoughtfully to one another and respond to the point, the "moving argument" may, and should, change course. This is always in response to the arguments that are set forth, the obstacles placed in the original path of thought. The purpose of the dialectical argument is not to advocate but to explore, not to demonstrate truth but to discover truth out of a process of contention and confrontation. The successful argument formed dialectically will deal with all possibilities and reach not a climax but a laconic conclusion: all things having been said, we end up here, rather than somewhere else.

The Rabbinic dialectical argument – the protracted, sometimes meandering, always moving flow of contentious thought – raises a question and answers it, then raises a question about the answer, and, having raised another question, it then gives an answer to that question and continues in the same fashion until a variety of issues has been sorted out. So it moves hither and yon; it is always one and coherent, but it is never the same, and it flows across the surface of the document at hand. The dialectical character derives not from the mere rhetorical device of question and answer, but from the pursuit of an argument, in a single line, though in many and diverse directions: not the form but the substantive continuity defines the criterion.

And the power of the dialectical argument flows from that continuity. We find the source of continuity in the author's capacity to show connections through the momentum of rigorous analysis, on the one side, and free-ranging curiosity, on the other.

Those second and third and fourth turnings therefore differentiate a dialectical from a static argument, much as the bubbles tell the difference between still and sparkling wine. The always-sparkling dialectical argument is one principal means by which the Talmud or some other Rabbinic writing accomplishes its goal of showing the connections between this and that, ultimately demonstrating the unity of many "thises and thats." What "moves" therefore is the flow of argument and thought, and that is – by definition – from problem to problem. The movement is generated specifically by the raising of contrary questions and theses. What characterizes the dialectical argument in Rabbinic literature is its meandering, its moving hither and yon. It is not a direct or straight-line movement, for example, the dialectical argument with which we are familiar in the modern West, thesis, antithesis, synthesis. It also does not correspond to any propositional or syllogistic argument, even though such arguments may take place in three or more steps, inclusive of counter-arguments.

Dialectical argument – the movement of thought through contentious challenge and passionate response, initiative and counter-ploy – thus characterizes the Talmud of Babylonia at its finest moments; though much in that Talmud, and still more in the prior Talmud of the Land of Israel, cannot qualify as dialectical at all. For the Talmud a dialectical argument is a systematic exposition, through give and take, moving from point to point, from a determinate starting point to an at-the-outset-indeterminate conclusion: wherever the challenge and response require that we go. In all the argument is the thing, since the dialectical argument routinely strays from its original, precipitating point and therefore does not undertake the demonstration so much as the exploration of a fixed proposition. Argument moves along, developing an idea through questions and answers, sometimes implicit, but more commonly explicit. That mode of analysis through media of question–answer and contentious argument imparts to the Talmud its distinctive and I should claim in its canonical context, unique characteristics of thought.[8] Called in the language of the Talmud *shaqla vetarya,* give and take, dialectics requires definition in neutral terms.

Earlier we claimed that the very specific character of the Mishnah defined the challenge that was met by the selection and utilization of the dialectical argument. What traits, exactly, lead sages to invent a mode of analysis lacking all precedent in prior Israelite writings to conduct the study of a document also lacking any sort of precedent? Two distinct reasons pertain.

First, a large-scale structure of lists, the Mishnah's generalizations rarely come to articulation; the mass of detail invited close study and analysis. The general had to emerge out of the concrete and specific, and generalizations valid at one point had to be tested against those emergent elsewhere; implications of generalizations for encompassing principles here required comparison and contrast with those that formed the foundations of a legal unit on an unrelated topic elsewhere. All of this work of construction would turn the Mishnah's details into large-scale compositions of encompassing significance. Proposals concerning the implicit principle in an articulated dispute, such as our claim in regard to Mishnah-tractate Uqsin 3:11, required close and sustained inspection – the testing of other possibilities, other interpretations altogether.

But, second, the Mishnah by itself did not exhaust the resources of normative rulings that formed the heritage of its time and sages. A sizable corpus of rulings in the name of Mishnah-authorities but not included in the Mishnah accompanied the Mishnah and contributed to the exposition of the law that it presents. And the Talmud, for its part, though organized around the Mishnah, in fact took as its problem the law of the Mishnah, along with other laws not found in the Mishnah but deriving from other, also authoritative sources. Here is the point at which the independence of judgment characteristic of the Talmudic sages, in the model of the Mishnaic sages, changed everything. In their view the law, not the document that contained it, dictated the course of inquiry.

The framers of the Mishnah made their choices – and the authors of the Talmud's principal dialectical arguments made theirs, extending to laws not included in the received code. The Talmud's sages accorded to the Mishnah a privileged position and made it the center of their exegetical writing. But this privileged position of the Mishnah did not extend to the laws that it set forth. If the framers of the Mishnah hoped to bring order out of chaos by giving the authoritative selection of the law – not merely a collection of their preferences and choices among laws – they were to find only disappointment. Repudiating the privileged position of the Mishnah, reducing the document to a mere framework for the organization of something greater, the writers of the Talmud's compositions and compilers of its composites redefined matters and assigned to themselves a far more important task than merely glossing a fixed code. They would deal with law deriving from all sources and do the work of criticism and harmonization that the diverse and conflicting laws made necessary.

That choice formed the Talmud's sages' response to a simple fact: the Mishnah collected only a small portion of the law that had come into being in the first and second centuries. A sizable corpus of opinion, rulings, cases and disputes, circulated from the period in which the Mishnah emerged but found (or was given) no place within the Mishnah. Some of these materials came to rest in the compilation of supplements to the Mishnah called the Tosefta. Corresponding to the Mishnah in its topical organization and program, the Tosefta exceeded it in sheer volume at least four times, perhaps more. Other laws were formulated along with attributions to the same authorities, Tannaite sages, who occur in the Mishnah. These laws scarcely differentiated themselves from those in the Mishnah, except in contents. Still more laws circulated, whether or not attributed to the names of authorities who occur also in the Mishnah, bearing the mark TNY – yielding "it was formulated as a Tannaite rule"[9] – and these too enjoyed the same standing and authority as Tannaite sayings collected in the Mishnah or the Tosefta.

If, therefore, a coherent and uniform, principled system of norms was to reach full articulation, the laws themselves, and not the Mishnah's limited selection of them, would form the arena for systematic study. That is to say, if a cogent system was to emerge out of the heritage of normative rulings out of Tannaite sponsorship, the entire mass of normative rulings would require analysis; points of contradiction would have to be sorted out; harmony between and among diverse laws would have to be established.

To accomplish not only the task of analysis of sayings, formulation and testing of generalizations, but, above all, the discovery of the principles embedded in the various, but normative rules governing discrete cases, the Talmud resorted to the dialectal argument. That would make possible the transformation of the Mishnah's lists, limited by their nature to data of a single kind, into the starting points for series capable of infinite extension across data of diverse kinds, as I shall explain in due course.

The implications of the character of the heritage of norms that our sages of blessed memory addressed with the Mishnah in hand prove self-evident. Specifically, had our sages of blessed memory received only the Mishnah, the character of that document would have imposed a labor of mere amplification of a well-crafted document and application of a uniform law. That is not only because of the exquisite quality of the craftsmanship exhibited in the Mishnah's composition, but also because of the pristine clarity of its laws themselves. Where there is a difference of opinion, it is labeled by assigning to the minority view a name, and with the majority, and normative, position given anonymously. So schism was signaled clearly, if tacitly. Hence applying the law would have imposed no formidable burdens. And had the Babylonian sages from the third to seventh centuries received only a mass of laws, deriving from hither and yon, the primary work of selection and organization, not analysis and theoretical synthesis, would have occupied their best energies. But that is not how matters worked out. The Mishnah imposed structure and order. The boundaries of discourse, therefore, were laid out. But the Mishnah's selectivity defined the exegetical problematics for further inquiry. Accordingly, our sages of blessed memory addressed a dual challenge, [1] both subjecting a well-crafted document to exegesis, amplification, and theoretical inquiry, but [2] also sorting out conflicting data on the same matters that said document took up.

A third trait of the Mishnah necessitated the formulation of an original mode of analytical argument. The Mishnah's character as a mass of petty rulings defined a task that was natural to the rigorous intellects who comprised the cadre of our sages of blessed memory. That was to require the quest not only for harmony but also generalization, the encompassing principle, the prevailing rule emerging from concrete data. For intellectuals of sages' sort sought not only information about details, but guidance on the main lines of thought. Not only so, but, engaged as they were in the administration of the life of the Jewish communities of Babylonia, theirs proved to be a practical reason and applied logic. They had not only to rule on cases covered by the Mishnah – and laws of its standing in addition – but also on cases not envisaged at all within the framework of the Mishnah. These cases of new kinds altogether, involving not only application of the law but penetration into the principles behind the law that could be made to cover new cases, demanded the formation of an analytical logic capable of generating principles to produce new laws.

And that is where dialectics entered in, for both practical and theoretical reasons. Theoretical considerations come first. Crafted, to begin with, to produce clarity of definition, the mode of dialectical argument of Classical philosophy defined a reliable method to secure compelling definitions of important principles. To deal with conflicting opinion on definition, two or more rulings on the same problem had to be set side by side and each was to be given its hearing. Perhaps the conflict could be resolved through making a distinction; in that case let one party challenge the other, with a harmonizing opinion then registering. Perhaps the conflict revealed principles that were at odds. These required articulation, analysis, juxtaposition and then, if possible, harmonization – reformulation at a higher level of abstraction.

Perhaps rulings on one topic rested on a principle that also affected rulings on another topic altogether. Then the principle expressed by rulings on that unrelated topic had to be made articulate and brought into relationship with the underlying principle operative elsewhere. And again, a given set of rulings served to illustrate a single point in common, and that point in common was to be formulated as a hypothesis of general intelligibility and applicability.

How better to test a hypothesis than in a dialogue between proponents and opponents, the latter raising contrary cases, the former overcoming contradiction, the former amplifying and extending their hypothesis, the latter proposing to limit it? The upshot is that the very character of the corpus of law received by our sages in Babylonia insured that a vast repertoire of conflict and contention would define the work of those responsible for the orderly application of the law – the Mishnah's law but not that alone – to the everyday affairs of the community of holy Israel.

Given the range of data to be addressed, the mode of question–answer, challenge out of conflicting data and response through resolution of conflict served as the principal medium of thought. The very character of the corpus of norms generated the kind of conflict best resolved through the challenge and response embodied in question-answer rhetoric of dialectics. The specific purpose of our sages' reading of the norms – the formulation of an internally coherent, proportionate, and harmonious statement – coincided with the promise of dialectic, which is to expose conflict and find ways through reason of resolving it. But if theory made dialectics the method of choice, politics re-enforced the theoretical usefulness of that method of thought and expression.

Moreover, practical considerations, both intellectual and political in character, underscored the usefulness of dialectics. Framed in a rhetoric aimed at effecting agreement out of conflict, preserving civility and rationality in confrontation of opinion, received tradition, or ideas, dialectics took a form exceedingly suitable to the situation of the sages. All of them proud, accomplished, certain of their knowledge, and opinionated, sages required a medium of thought that would accord recognition and respect to all participants. Simply announcing opinions – solutions to problems, rulings on cases, theories for analytical consideration – accomplished little when the participants to public discourse addressed one another as equals and laid a heavy claim upon a full hearing for their respective views.

And even had our sages proved men of limited intellect, politics pointed toward dialogue and argued in favor of a rhetoric of dialectics. Few possessed access to coercive force,[10] other than that of intellectual power and moral authority. For, lacking an efficient administration capable of imposing order, they could hope to accomplish their goals through persuasion, not coercion. Denied the services of a police force or army, effective principally through public opinion and persuasion (relying heavily, for instance, upon ostracism as a social penalty), our sages could best impose their will by means of powerful argument. The power of rationality, moreover, proved singularly congruent to sages' circumstance, since none of them enjoyed political sponsorship sufficient to compel the rest to conform, and all of the more influential ones jealously guarded their standing and prerogatives.

Now let us turn to a concrete example of the Talmud's dialectical argument. The first passage that we consider occurs at the Babylonian Talmud Baba Mesia 5B–6A, which is to say, Talmud to Mishnah Baba Mesia 1:1–2, the Mishnah-paragraphs we have already met in Chapter 1. In the translation that follows, bold typeface reproduces a passage of the Mishnah or Tosefta, plain type, a passage in Hebrew, and italics, a passage in Aramaic. As we shall see, Aramaic bears the burden of argument; the dialectics is always in Aramaic. Our interest is in the twists and turns of the argument. We now have to discern what is at stake in the formation of a continuous and unfolding composition:

> **[5B] IV.1. A. This one takes an oath that he possesses no less a share of it than half, [and that one takes an oath that he possesses no less a share of it than half, and they divide it up]**

The rule of the Mishnah, which is cited at the head of the sustained discussion, concerns the case of two persons who find a garment. We settle their conflicting claim by requiring each to take an oath that he or she owns title to no less than half of the garment, and then we split the garment between them.

Our first question is one of text-criticism: analysis of the Mishnah-paragraph's word choice. We say that the oath concerns the portion that the claimant alleges he possesses. But the oath really affects the portion that he does not have in hand at all:

[B] *Is it concerning the portion that he claims he possesses that he takes the oath, or concerning the portion that he does not claim to possess?* [Daiches: "The implication is that the terms of the oath are ambiguous. By swearing that his share in it is not "less than half," the claimant might mean that it is not even a third or a fourth (which is "less than half"), and the negative way of putting it would justify such an interpretation. He could therefore take this oath even if he knew that he had no share in the garment at all, while he would be swearing falsely if he really had a share in the garment that is less than half, however small that share might be.]

[C] *Said R. Huna, "It is that he says, 'By an oath! I possess in it a portion, and I possess in it a portion that is no more than half a share of it.'"* [The claimant swears that his share is at least half (Daiches, *Baba Mesia, ad loc.*).]

Having asked and answered the question, we now find ourselves in an extension of the argument; the principal trait of the dialectical argument is now before us: [1] but [2] maybe the contrary is the case, so [3] what about – that is, the setting aside of a proposition in favor of its opposite. Here we come to the definitive trait of the dialectical argument: its insistence on challenging every proposal with the claim, "maybe it's the opposite?" This pestering question forces us back upon our sense of self-evidence; it makes us consider the contrary to each position we propose to set forth. It makes thought happen. True, the Talmud's voice "but" – the whole of the dialectic in one word! – presents a formidable nuisance. But so does all criticism, and only the mature mind will welcome criticism. Dialectics is not for children, politicians, propagandists, or egoists. Genuine curiosity about the truth shown by rigorous logic forms the counterpart to musical virtuosity. So the objection proceeds:

[C] *Then let him say,* "By an oath! The whole of it is mine!"

Why claim half when the alleged finder may as well demand the whole cloak?

> [D] *But are we going to give him the whole of it?* [Obviously not, there is another claimant, also taking an oath.]

The question contradicts the facts of the case: two parties claim the cloak, so the outcome can never be that one will get the whole thing.

> [E] *Then let him say,* "By an oath! Half of it is mine!"

Then – by the same reasoning – why claim "no less than half," rather than simply, half.

> [F] *That would damage his own claim* [which was that he owned the whole of the cloak, not only half of it].

The claimant does claim the whole cloak, so the proposed language does not serve to replicate his actual claim. That accounts for the language that is specified.

> [G] *But here too is it not the fact that, in the oath that he is taking, he impairs his own claim?* [After all, he here makes explicit the fact that he owns at least half of it. What happened to the other half?]

The solution merely compounds the problem.

> [H] *[Not at all.] For he has said,* "The whole of it is mine!" [And, he further proceeds,] "And as to your contrary view, By an oath, I do have a share in it, and that share is no less than half!"

We solve the problem by positing a different solution from the one we suggested at the outset. Why not start where we have concluded? Because if we had done so, we should have ignored a variety of intervening considerations and so should have expounded less than the entire range of possibilities. The power of the dialectical argument now is clear: it forces us to address not the problem and the solution alone, but the problem and the various ways by which a solution may be reached; then, when we do come to a final solution to the question at hand, we have reviewed all of the possibilities. We have seen how everything flows together, nothing is left unattended.

What we have here is not a set piece of two positions, with an analysis of each, such as that the formal dialogue, as we saw in

Chapter 1, exposes with such elegance; it is, rather, an analytical argument, explaining why this, not that, then why not that but rather this; and onward to the other thing and the thing beyond that – a linear argument in constant forward motion. When we speak of a moving argument, this is what we mean: what is not static and merely expository, but what is dynamic and always contentious. It is not an endless argument, an argument for the sake of arguing, or evidence that what is important to the Talmud and other writings that use the dialectics as a principal mode of dynamic argument is process but not position. To the contrary, the passage is resolved with a decisive conclusion, not permitted to run on.

But the dialectical composition proceeds – continuous and coherent from point to point, even as it zigs and zags. We proceed to the second cogent proposition in the analysis of the cited Mishnah-passage, which asks a fresh question: why an oath at all?

[2A] [It is envisioned that each party is holding on to a corner of the cloak, so the question is raised:] Now, since this one is possessed of the cloak and standing right there, and that one is possessed of the cloak and is standing right there, why in the world do I require this oath?

Until now we have assumed as fact the premise of the Mishnah's rule, which is that an oath is there to be taken. But why assume so? Surely each party now has what he is going to get. So what defines the point and effect of the oath?

[B] Said R. Yohanan, "This oath [to which our Mishnah-passage refers] happens to be an ordinance imposed only by rabbis,

[C] "so that people should not go around grabbing the cloaks of other people and saying, 'It's mine!'" [But, as a matter of fact, the oath that is imposed in our Mishnah-passage is not legitimate by the law of the Torah. It is an act taken by sages to maintain the social order.]

We do not administer oaths to liars; we do not impose an oath in a case in which one of the claimants would take an oath for something he knew to be untrue, since one party really does own the cloak, the other really has grabbed it. The proposition solves the problem – but is hardly going to settle the question. On the contrary, Yohanan raises more problems than he solves. So we ask how we can agree to an oath in this case at all?

[D] *But why then not advance the following argument: since such a one is suspect as to fraud in a property claim, he also should be suspect as to fraud in oath-taking?*

Yohanan places himself into the position of believing in respect to the oath what we will not believe in respect to the claim on the cloak, for, after all, one of the parties before us must be lying! Why sustain such a contradiction: gullible and suspicious at one and the same time?

[E] *In point of fact, we do not advance the argument: since such a one is suspect as to fraud in a property claim, he also should be suspect as to fraud in oath-taking, for if you do not concede that fact, then how is it possible that the All-Merciful has ruled,* "One who has conceded part of a claim against himself must take an oath as to the remainder of what is subject to claim?"

If someone claims that another party holds property belonging to him or her, and the one to whom the bailment has been handed over for safe-keeping, called the bailee, concedes part of the claim, the bailee must then take an oath in respect to the rest of the claimed property, that is, the part that the bailee maintains does not belong to the claimant at all. So the law itself – the Torah, in fact – has sustained the same contradiction. That fine solution, of course, is going to be challenged:

[F] *Why not simply maintain, since such a one is suspect as to fraud in a property claim, he also should be suspect as to fraud in oath-taking?*

[G] *In that other case, [the reason for the denial of part of the claim and the admission of part is not the intent to commit fraud, but rather,] the defendant is just trying to put off the claim for a spell.*

We could stop at this point without losing a single important point of interest; everything is before us. One of the striking traits of the large-scale dialectical composition is its composite character. Starting at the beginning, without any loss of meaning or sense, we may well stop at the end of any given paragraph of thought. But the dialectics insists on moving forward, exploring, pursuing, insisting; and were we to remove a paragraph in the middle of a dialectical composite, then all that follows would become incomprehensible. That is a mark of the dialectical argument: sustained, continuous, and coherent – yet perpetually in control and capable of resolving matters at any single point. For those of us who consume, but do not produce, arguments of such dynamism and complexity, the task is to discern the continuity, that is to say, not to lose sight of where we stand in the whole movement.

Now, having fully exposed the topic, its problem, and its principles, we take a tangent indicated by the character of the principle before us: when a person will or will not lie or take a false oath. We have a theory on the matter; what we will now do is expound the theory, with special reference to the formulation of that theory in explicit terms by a named authority:

[H] This concurs with the position of Rabbah. [For Rabbah has said, "On what account has the Torah imposed the requirement of an oath on one who confesses to only part of a claim against him? It is by reason of the presumption that a person will not insolently deny the truth about the whole of a loan in the very presence of the creditor and so entirely deny the debt. He will admit to part of the debt and deny part of it. Hence we invoke an oath in a case in which one does so, to coax out the truth of the matter."]

[I] For you may know, [in support of the foregoing], that R. Idi bar Abin said R. Hisda [said]: "He who [falsely] denies owing money on a loan nonetheless is suitable to give testimony, but he who denies that he holds a bailment for another party cannot give testimony."

The proposition is now fully exposed. A named authority is introduced, who will concur in the proposed theoretical distinction. He sets forth an extra-logical consideration, which of course the law always will welcome: the rational goal of finding the truth overrides the technicalities of the law governing the oath.

Predictably, we cannot allow matters to stand without challenge, and the challenge comes at a fundamental level, with the predictable give-and-take to follow:

[J] But what about that which R. Ammi bar. Hama repeated on Tannaite authority: "[If they are to be subjected to an oath,] four sorts of bailees have to have denied part of the bailment and conceded part of the bailment, namely, the unpaid bailee, the borrower, the paid bailee, and the one who rents."

[K] *Why not simply maintain, since such a one is suspect as to fraud in a property claim, he also should be suspect as to fraud in oath-taking?*

[L] *In that case as well, [the reason for the denial of part of the claim and the admission of part is not the intent to commit fraud, but rather,] the defendant is just trying to put off the claim for a spell.*

[M] *He reasons as follows: "I'm going to find the thief and arrest him." Or: "I'll find [the beast] in the field and return it to the owner."*

Once more, "if that is the case" provokes yet another analysis; we introduce a different reading of the basic case before us, another reason that we should not impose an oath:

[N] *If that is the case, then why should one who denies holding a bailment ever be unsuitable to give testimony? Why don't we just maintain that the defendant is just trying to put off the claim for a spell. He reasons as follows: "I'm going to look for the thing and find it."*

[O] *When in point of fact we do rule,* He who denies holding a bailment is unfit to give testimony, *it is in a case in which witnesses come and give testimony against him that at that very moment, the bailment is located in the bailee's domain, and he fully is informed of that fact, or, alternatively, he has the object in his possession at that very moment.*

The solution to the problem at hand also provides the starting point for yet another step in the unfolding exposition. Huna has given us a different resolution of matters. That accounts for number 3, and number 4 is also predictable:

[3A] *But as to that which R. Huna has said* [when we have a bailee who offers to pay compensation for a lost bailment rather than swear it has been lost, since he wishes to appropriate the article by paying for it, (Daiches)], "They impose upon him the oath that the bailment is not in his possession at all,"

[B] *why not in that case invoke the principle, since such a one is suspect as to fraud in a property claim, he also should be suspect as to fraud in oath-taking?*

[C] *In that case also, he may rule in his own behalf, I'll give him the money.*

[4A] *Said R. Aha of Difti to Rabina, "But then the man clearly transgresses the negative commandment: 'You shall not covet.'"*

[B] "*You shall not covet" is generally understood by people to pertain to something for which one is not ready to pay.*

Yet another authority's position is now invoked, and it draws us back
to our starting point: the issue of why we think an oath is suitable in
a case in which we ought to assume lying is going on; so we are
returned to our starting point, but via a circuitous route:

[5A] [6A] *But as to that which R. Nahman said,* "They impose
upon him [who denies the whole of a claim] an oath of
inducement," *why not in that case invoke the principle, since
such a one is suspect as to fraud in a property claim, he also
should be suspect as to fraud in oath-taking?*

[B] *And furthermore, there is that which R. Hiyya taught on
Tannaite authority:* "Both parties [employee, supposed to have
been paid out of an account set up by the employer at a local
store, and store-keeper] take an oath and collect what each
claims from the employer," *why not in that case invoke the
principle, since such a one is suspect as to fraud in a property
claim, he also should be suspect as to fraud in oath-taking?*

[C] *And furthermore, there is that which R. Sheshet said,* "We
impose upon an unpaid bailee [who claims that the animal
has been lost] three distinct oaths: first, an oath that I have
not deliberately caused the loss, that I did not put a hand on
it, and that it is not in my domain at all," *why not in that case
invoke the principle, since such a one is suspect as to fraud in a
property claim, he also should be suspect as to fraud in oath-
taking?*

We now settle the matter:

[D] *It must follow that we do not invoke the principle at all, since such
a one is suspect as to fraud in a property claim, he also should be
suspect as to fraud in oath-taking?*

What is interesting is why walk so far to end up where we started: do
we invoke said principle? No, we do not.

What we have accomplished on our wanderings is a survey of opinion on a theme, to be sure, but opinion that intersects at our
particular problem as well. The moving argument serves to carry us
hither and yon; its power is to demonstrate that all considerations are
raised, all challenges met, all possibilities explored. This is not merely
a set-piece argument, where we have proposition, evidence, analysis,
conclusion; it is a different sort of thinking altogether, purposive and
coherent, but also comprehensive and compelling for its admission of
possibilities and attention to alternatives. The dialectical argument

supplies the Talmud's medium of generalization from case to principle and extension from principle to new cases.

First, we test every allegation by a counter-proposition, so serving the cause of truth through challenge and constant checking for flaws in an argument.

Second, we survey the entire range of possibilities, which leaves no doubts about the cogency of our conclusion. And that means, we move out of our original case, guided by its generative principle to new cases altogether.

Third, quite to the point, by the give and take of argument, we ourselves are enabled to go through the thought processes set forth in the subtle markings that yield our reconstruction of the argument. We not only review what people say, but how they think: the processes of reasoning that have yielded a given conclusion. Sages and disciples become party to the modes of thought; in the dialectical argument, they are required to replicate the thought-processes themselves.

For a second, and final example, let us give a single instance of the power of the dialectical argument to expose the steps in thinking that lead from one end to another: principle to ruling, or ruling to principle. In the present instance, the only one we require to see a perfectly routine and obvious procedure, we mean to prove the point that if people are permitted to obstruct the public way, if damage was done by them, they are liable to pay compensation. First, we are going to prove that general point on the basis of a single case. Then we shall proceed to show how a variety of authorities, dealing with diverse cases, sustain the same principle.

[O] **He who brings out his manure to the public domain –**

[P] **while one party pitches it out, the other party must be bringing it in to manure his field.**

[Q] **They do not soak clay in the public domain,**

[R] **and they do not make bricks.**

[S] **And they knead clay in the public way,**

[T] **but not bricks.**

[U] **He who builds in the public way –**

[V] **while one party brings stones, the builder must make use of them in the public way.**

[W] **And if one has inflicted injury, he must pay for the damages he has caused.**

[X] **Rabban Simeon b. Gamaliel says, "Also: He may prepare**

for doing his work [on site in the public way] for thirty days [before the actual work of building]."

(Talmud Baba Mesia 10:5/O–X)

We begin with the comparison of the rule before us with another Tannaite position on the same issue, asking whether an unattributed, therefore authoritative, rule stands for or opposes the position of a given authority; we should hope to prove that the named authority concurs. So one fundamental initiative in showing how many cases express a single principle – the concrete demonstration of the unity of the law – is to find out whether diverse, important authorities concur on the principle, each ruling in a distinctive case; or whether a single authority is consistent in ruling in accord with the principle at hand, as in what follows:

[I.1A] *May we say that our Mishnah-paragraph does not accord with the view of R. Judah? For it has been taught on Tannaite authority:*

[B] **R. Judah says, "At the time of fertilizing the fields, a man may take out his manure and pile it up at the door of his house in the public way so that it will be pulverized by the feet of man and beast, for a period of thirty days. For it was on that very stipulation that Joshua caused the Israelites to inherit the land" [T.B.M. 11:8E–H].**

[C] You may even maintain that he concurs with the Mishnah's rule [that while one party pitches it out, the other party must be bringing it in to manure his field]. R. Judah concedes that if one has caused damage, he is liable to pay compensation.

In line with the position just now proposed, then Judah will turn out to rule every which way on the same matter. And that is not an acceptable upshot.

[D] *But has it not been taught in the Mishnah:* **If the store-keeper had left his lamp outside the store-keeper is liable [if the flame caused a fire]. R. Judah said, "In the case of a lamp for Hanukkah, he is exempt" [M.B.Q. 6:6E–F],** because he has acted under authority. *Now surely that must mean,* under the authority of the court [and that shows that one is not responsible for damage caused by his property in the public domain if it was there under the authority of the court]!

66

The dialectic now intervenes. We have made a proposal. Isn't it a good one? Of course not, were we to give up so quickly, we should gain nothing:

[E] *No, what it means is, on the authority of carrying out one's religious obligations.*

By now, the reader is able to predict the next step: "but isn't the contrary more reasonable?" Here is how we raise the objection.

[F] *But has it not been taught on Tannaite authority:*

[G] in the case of all those concerning whom they have said, "They are permitted to obstruct the public way," if there was damage done, one is liable to pay compensation. But R. Judah declares one exempt from having to pay compensation.

[H] *So it is better to take the view that our Mishnah-paragraph does not concur with the position of R. Judah.*

The point of interest has been introduced: whether those permitted to obstruct the public way must pay compensation for damages they may cause in so doing. Here is where we find a variety of cases that yield a single principle:

[2A] Said Abayye, "R. Judah, Rabban Simeon b. Gamaliel, and R. Simeon all take the position that in the case of all those concerning whom they have said, 'They are permitted to obstruct the public way,' if there was damage done, one is liable to pay compensation.

[B] *As to R. Judah, the matter is just as we have now stated it.*

Simeon b. Gamaliel and Simeon now draw us to unrelated cases:

[C] *As to Rabban Simeon b. Gamaliel, we have learned in the Mishnah:* "**Rabban Simeon b. Gamaliel says, 'Also: He may prepare for doing his work [on site in the public way] for thirty days [before the actual work of building].'**

[D] *As to R. Simeon, we have learned in the Mishnah:* **A person should not set up an oven in a room unless there is a space of four cubits above it. If he was setting it up in the upper story, there has to be a layer of plaster under it three handbreadths thick, and in the case of a stove, a handbreadth thick. And if it did damage, the owner of the oven has to pay for the damage. R. Simeon says, 'All of these measures have been stated only so that if the object did damage, the**

owner is exempt from paying compensation if the stated measures have been observed' [M.B.B. 2:2A–F]."

We see then that the demonstration of the unity of the law and the issue of who stands, or does not stand, behind a given rule, go together. When we ask about who does or does not stand behind a rule, we ask about the principle of a case, which leads us downward to a premise, and we forthwith point to how that same premise underlies a different principle yielding a case – so how can X hold the view he does, if that is his premise, since at a different case he makes a point with a principle that rests on a contradictory premise. The Mishnah and the Talmud are comparable to the moraine left by the last ice age, fields studded with boulders. For the Talmud, reference is made to those many disputes that litter the pages and impede progress. That explains why much of the Talmud is taken up with not only sorting out disputes, but also showing their rationality, meaning that reasonable people have perfectly valid reasons for disagreeing about a given point, since both parties share the same premises but apply them differently; or they really do not differ at all, since one party deals with one set of circumstances, the other with a different set of circumstances.

Dialectics empowers the disciple of the sages to join in the conversation by showing not only the result but the workings of the logical mind. By following dialectical arguments, we ourselves enter into those same thought processes, and our minds then are formed in the model of rigorous and sustained, systematic argument. The reason is simply stated. When we follow a proposal and its refutation, the consequence thereof, and the result of that, we ourselves form partners to the logical tensions and their resolutions; we are given an opening into the discourse that lies before us. As soon as matters turn not upon tradition, to which we may or may not have access, but reason, specifically, challenge and response, proposal and counter-proposal, "maybe matters are just the opposite?", we find an open door before us.

For these are not matters of fact but of reasoned judgment, and the answer, "well, that's my opinion," in its "traditional form," namely, that is what Rabbi X has said so that must be so, finds no hearing. Moving from facts to reasoning, propositions to the process of counter-argument, the challenge resting on the mind's own movement, its power of manipulating facts one way rather than some other and of identifying the governing logic of a fact – that process invites the reader's or the listener's participation. The author of a dialectical composite presents a problem with its internal tensions in logic and offers a solution to the problem and a resolution of the logical conflicts.

What is at stake in the capacity of the framer of a composite, or even the author of a composition, to move this way and that, always in a continuous path, but often in a crooked one? The dialectical argument opens the possibility of reaching out from one thing to something else, and the path's wandering is part of the reason. It is not because people have lost sight of their starting point or their goal in the end, but because they want to encompass, in the analytical argument as it gets underway, as broad and comprehensive a range of cases and rules as they can. The movement from point to point in reference to a single point that accurately describes the dialectical argument reaches a goal of abstraction. At the point at which we leave behind the specificities not only of cases but laws, sages carry the argument upward to the law that governs many cases, the premises that undergird many rules, and still higher to the principles that infuse diverse premises; then the principles that generate other, unrelated premises, which, in turn, come to expression in other, still less intersecting cases. The meandering course of argument comes to an end when we have shown how things cohere that we did not even imagine were contiguous at all.

The mode of argument made possible through dialectics – two or more positions fully exposed, with arguments pro and con, a complete repertoire of positions and possibilities, laid out in the form of an exchange between and among equals, with point-by-point *Auseindersetzungen*, allowing for the full articulation of generalizations, exceptions based on cases, counter-arguments, and competing generalizations – that mode of argument alone could prove congruent to the politics of powerful intellects lacking worldly position to sustain their hypotheses. Accordingly, our sages chose wisely when they determined that argument in dialogic form, within dialectical logic, defined the best possible instrument with which to accomplish their task of explanation, analysis, and amplification of the law that they had received not only from the Mishnah but from other sources of the same status or origin. So much for the mode of argument. What can we say of its character and substance?

4

CONDUCTING DIALECTICAL ARGUMENT IN ORIGEN

THE GLOBAL IMPLICATIONS OF PAUL'S PROGRESSIVE DIALECTICS

The discussion in Chapter 2 has enabled us to see that dialectics were embedded in Paul's interpretation of Scripture. His identification of antitheses there, together with a progressive argument which pointed to the experience of Spirit within the community as that which resolved the conflicts, constitutes his major contribution to Christian theology. It is even more important than his teaching of righteousness by means of faith, because his interpretative method is what made it possible for him to frame and to argue his distinctive doctrine of justification.

Generally speaking, Paul's evolution of progressive dialectics occurred *within* his interpretation of Scriptures, and his method did not involve the claim that his interpretation replaced the authority of Scriptures as such. That development, as we have also seen, awaited the Epistle to the Hebrews. Even at the stage of Hebrews, however, and for some time thereafter, Christian dialectics remained rooted in an explicit discussion of the Scriptures of Israel.

Yet the implicit claim of progressive dialectics in the manner of Paul is that any object of concern, viewed under the aspect of the cross, will ultimately yield to the identification of antinomies, and their spiritual resolution. That was the promise of a truly dialectical theology, because the claim was in fact global: that "God was reconciling us to himself through Christ, and giving us the ministry of reconciliation" (so 2 Cor. 5:18). Paul pursued that thought to its logical conclusion, that the reconciliation involved was inherently cosmic in scope:

As God was in Christ reconciling the world to himself, not attributing their transgressions to them, he established in us the word of reconciliation. Therefore we are envoys on behalf of Christ, as God is appealing through us: we beseech on Christ's behalf, be reconciled to God. For our sake he made the one who did not know sin into sin, so that we might become the righteousness of God in him.

(2 Cor. 5:19–20)

Paul is here compressing the hermeneutics of Gal. 3 (discussed in Chapter 2) into a succinct statement, and then using that theory to account for the contemporary realization of atonement. In principle, nothing within human awareness could escape the hermeneutics of the cross.

Progressive dialectics had led – practically as soon as they were applied to the Torah – to a distinctively Pauline understanding of ethics (again, see Chapter 2). The shift in the role of all law (from central regulation to ancillary attestation of promise) meant that the impetus of the Spirit had replaced the constraint of the Torah as the primary ethical principle. The fields of Scripture and of ethics were natural places for Paul's progressive dialectics to be worked out, because they were already fraught with controversy. In principle, however, Paul opened the way for the global application of his hermeneutics, as an interpretation of human experience generally.

In what follows, we will see how – in a specific discussion – Paul opened the way for a more consistently dialectical approach to human experience, without necessary reference to the Scriptures or ethics. The issue Paul engaged was the resurrection of the dead. It was a particular concern in Corinth, and therefore may be viewed as Paul's address of an occasional, local anxiety. But the very nature of the question, involving both anthropology and eschatology, takes Paul into the realm of a dialectical inquiry without Scriptural or ethical boundaries. That brief foray into unbridled theological dialectics was taken as a vital opportunity nearly two centuries later by Origen. In Origen's analysis of both human and divine nature, dialectics became the central engine of all theological inquiry. The seal of his influence, and the importance of his contribution, may be seen in the crucial place dialectics have played in the understanding of the Trinity.

THE DIALECTICS OF THE RESURRECTION IN PAUL

Paul's discussion of the issue of the resurrection in 1 Cor. 15 clearly represents his continuing commitment to his dialectical and progressive principles, even outside the realm of Scripture. The particular occasion of his teaching is the denial of the resurrection on the part of some people in Corinth (1 Cor. 15:12b): "how can some of you say that there is no resurrection of the dead?" His address of that denial is, initially, on the basis of the integrity of apostolic preaching. Indeed, Paul precedes his question with the earliest extant record of the traditions regarding Jesus' resurrection (1 Corinthians 15:1–11). That enables Paul to press on to his first argument against the Corinthian denial of the resurrection (15:13–14): "But if there is no resurrection of the dead, neither has Christ been raised; and if Christ has not been raised, then our preaching is empty and your faith is empty!"

Paul expands on this argument in what follows (1 Cor. 15:15–19), but the gist of what he says in that section is as simple as what he says at the outset: faith in Jesus' resurrection requires our affirmation of the reality of resurrection generally. That may seem to be an argument entirely from hypothesis, until we recall (as we have already seen in Chapter 2) that Paul sees the moment when belief in Jesus occurs as the occasion of our reception of the Spirit of God:

> When the fullness of time came, God sent forth his Son, born from woman, born under law, so that he might redeem those under law, in order that we might obtain Sonship. And because you are sons, God sent the Spirit of his Son into our hearts, crying, "Abba! Father!"
>
> (Gal. 4:4–6)

Because the Spirit in baptism is nothing other than the Spirit of God's Son, Jesus' resurrection is attested by the very fact of the primordial Christian experience. The availability of his Spirit shows that he has been raised from the dead. In addition, the preaching in his name formally claims his resurrection, so that to deny resurrection as a whole is to make the apostolic preaching into a lie: empty preaching, as Paul says, and therefore empty faith.

His emphasis on the spiritual integrity of the apostolic preaching, attested in baptismal experience, enables Paul to proceed to portray Jesus as the first of those raised from the dead. His resurrection is what provides hope for the resurrection of the dead as a whole (1 Cor. 15:20–28). That hope, Paul goes on to argue, is what permits the Corinthians themselves to engage in the practice of being baptized on behalf of the dead (15:29).[1] The practice assumes that, when the dead come to be raised, even if they have not been baptized during life, baptism on their behalf after their death will confer benefit. Similarly, Paul takes his own courage as an example of the hopeful attitude which must assume the resurrection of the dead as its ground: why else would Christians encounter the dangers that they do (15:30–32a)?

The last phase of Paul's argument on the basis of the practice and the hope of faith in the resurrection is that a denial of the resurrection corrupts the life of the community (1 Cor. 15:32–34): "'Let us eat and drink, for we die tomorrow.' Do not be deceived: 'bad associations corrupt the good.'" What is interesting here is that Paul is using a dialectical argument on the basis of the Greek literary tradition. The first maxim is echoed in many places (for instance in Euripides' *Acestis* 781–889), and is juxtaposed to the second, from a play of Menander (*Thais*). Paul is doing to the advice to enjoy mortal pleasures what he has already done (for example) to the command to perform circumcision: it is effectively reversed in the face of what Paul takes to be the governing intent of the writing. Just as the function of the Torah is to lead one to be baptized, rather than to regulate one's behavior, so the function of the Hellenistic literary tradition is to produce refined associations, not corrupt ones. If the advice seems to be towards corruption, it is not to be taken at face value, any more than the command to perform circumcision (for instance) is to be taken literally.

Paul's dialectical reading of Euripides and Menander leads on to a trenchant conclusion, the cap of this section of his argument (1 Cor. 15:34): "Come around to your senses, and sin no more. Some have no knowledge of God: I speak to your shame." The postulate on which Paul has been operating, throughout the argument in Chapter 15, is that the Spirit in baptism, known to believers generally, pursues its own logic. That logic excludes corrupt behavior, and the hopelessness which feeds corruption. It is a logic of affect and deed as well as of proposition, such that the proposition that Christ has been raised from the dead, one's own hope of resurrection, and commitment to ethical conduct, are all integrated within a single dialectic. And the demonstration of the dialectic can come from Euripides and Menander, as well as from Leviticus and Habakkuk (as in Galatians).

But a claim of resurrection does not only involve a hope based upon a reception of Spirit and the hopeful dialectics of Scriptures, whether Judaic or Hellenistic. Resurrection as a statement logically impinges upon what becomes of persons as we actually know them after they have died. Paul's argument therefore can not and does not rest solely on assertions of the spiritual integrity of the apostolic preaching and of the testimony of ancient authorities. He must also spell out an anthropology of resurrection, such that the spiritual hope and the Scriptural witness are worked out within the terms of reference of human experience. Precisely when he does that in 1 Cor. 15, Paul develops a Christian metaphysics. He makes that startling contribution because he applies the dialectic approach he developed for interpretative purposes to the terms of reference of what makes for a human being.

When Paul thinks of a person, he conceives of a body as composed of flesh, physical substance which varies from one created thing to another (for example, people, animals, fish, and birds; 1 Cor. 15:35–39). But in addition to being physical bodies, people are also what Paul calls a "psychic body," that is, bodies with souls (1 Cor. 15:44). (Unfortunately, the phrase is wrongly translated in many modern versions, but its dependence on the noun for "soul" [*psukhe*] is obvious. The adjective does not mean "physical" as we use that word.) In other words, people as bodies are not just lumps of flesh, but they are self-aware. That self-awareness is precisely what makes them "psychic body."

Now in addition to being physical body and psychic body, Paul says we are (or can be, within the power of resurrection) "spiritual body" (1 Cor. 15:44): "it is sown a psychic body, it is raised a spiritual body." That is, we can relate thoughts and feelings *to one another and to God.* The explanation of how spirit may be the medium of God's communication is developed earlier in 1 Cor. (2:10–11). Paul develops his position by quoting a passage from Isa. 64:4 (in 2:9), which speaks of things beyond human understanding which God has readied for those who love him, and Paul then goes on to say:

> God has revealed them to us through the Spirit; for the Spirit searches all things, even the depths of God. For who knows a person's affairs except the person's spirit within? So also no one has known God's affairs except the Spirit of God.
>
> (1 Cor. 2:10–11)

As Paul sees human relations, one person can only know what another thinks and feels on the basis of their shared "spirit." "Spirit" is the name for what links one person with another, and by means of that link we can also know what God thinks and feels. The spirit at issue then, Paul goes on to say, is not "the spirit of the world," but "the Spirit from God" (1 Cor. 2:12): the medium of ordinary, human exchange becomes in baptism the vehicle of divine revelation.

Paul's remark in 1 Cor. 2 is part of a complete anthropology, which is spelled out further in 1 Cor. 15. Jesus on the basis of the resurrection is the last Adam, a life-giving spirit (1 Cor. 15:45) just as the first Adam was a living being or soul (the two words are the same in Greek, *psukhe*). Jesus is the basis on which we can realize our identities as God's children, the brothers and sisters of Christ, and know the power of the resurrection. In so saying, Paul defines a distinctive christology as well as a characteristic spirituality. The metaphysics of both, which relate Christ to creation and believers to God, is predicated upon a dialectical treatment of human nature. "Flesh" and "soul" become, not ends in themselves, but way-stations on the way to "spirit."

ORIGEN AND THE EXPANSIVE REFINEMENT OF DIALECTICS

Born in 185 in Egypt, Origen knew the consequences which faith could have in the Roman world: his father died during the persecution of Severus in 202. Origen accepted the sort of renunciation demanded of apostles in the Gospels, putting aside his possessions to develop what Eusebius calls the philosophical life demanded by Jesus (see Eusebius, *History of the Church* 6.3). His learning resulted in his appointment to the catechetical school in Alexandria, following the great examples of Pantaenus and Clement. Origen later moved to Caesarea in Palestine, as a result of a bitter dispute with Demetrius, the bishop of Alexandria. Indeed, Origen remained a controversial figure after his death (and until this day), to a large extent because he wrestled more profoundly than most thinkers with the consequences of Spirit's claim on the flesh.

The dispute surrounding Origen specifically included his sexuality. According to Eusebius, as part of his acceptance of evangelical precepts of renunciation, Origen took literally the reference in Matthew to people making eunuchs of themselves for the sake of the kingdom of heaven (Mat. 19:12). Accordingly, he emasculated himself (*History of the Church* 6.8). As Eusebius immediately goes on to say, Demetrius later capitalized on the story, by using it to discredit Origen. Scholarship has been divided over the question of whether Origen in fact castrated himself.

The scholarly debate about Origen's genitals is less interesting than the fact that there has been such a debate. If Origen did castrate himself, the argument has been (since the time of Eusebius!), that it must have been because his interpretation of Scripture was literal at that stage of his life. If he did not, Demetrius must have invented the story. Castration is the extreme and negative form of the celibacy encouraged and required within Christian circles from the second century onward; the physical cutting crosses the line between renunciation and mutilation. Whether the act is taken to have been performed on Origen's body or only in Demetrius's mind, no one defends it. The story about Origen violates the axiom (articulated by Paul in 1 Cor. 6:19) that the human body, as an actual or potential vehicle of the divine, is not to be desecrated.

In fact, Origen himself argued against any literal interpretation of Mat. 19:12, insisting that it did not refer to self-mutilation.[2] The passage has been used to suggest that Origen did castrate himself, and later saw the error of the act, as well as to argue that he never would have done such a thing. The matter is not likely ever to be settled, but what Origen did settle to his own satisfaction was the fraught issue of the relationship between flesh and spirit, the tension between which produced the plausibility of the claim that a great Christian teacher might castrate himself. But where the reputation of Origen has been stalled in the antithesis between flesh and spirit, his own thought was productive precisely because he worked out a dialectical reconciliation between the two.

In his treatment of the resurrection, Origen shows himself a brilliant exegete and a profound theologian. He sees clearly that, in 1 Cor. 15, Paul insists that the resurrection from the dead must be bodily. And Origen provides the logical grounding of Paul's claim:

> If it is certain that we are to be possessed of bodies, and if those bodies that have fallen are declared to rise again – and the expression "rise again" could not properly be used except of that which had previously fallen – then there can be no doubt that these bodies rise again in order that at the resurrection we may once more be clothed with them.
>
> (*On First Principles* 2.10.1)

But Origen equally insists upon Paul's assertion that "flesh and blood can not inherit the kingdom of God" (1 Cor. 15:50). There must be a radical transition from flesh to spirit, as God fashions a body which can dwell in the heavens (*On First Principles* 2.10.3).

Origen pursues the point of this transition into a debate with fellow Christians:

We now direct the discussion to some of our own people, who either from want of intellect or from lack of instruction introduce an exceedingly low and mean idea of the resurrection of the body. We ask these men in what manner they think that the "psychic body" will, by the grace of the resurrection, be changed and become "spiritual;" and in what manner they think that what is sown "in dishonor" is to "rise in glory," and what is sown "in corruption" is to be transformed into "incorruption." Certainly if they believe the Apostle, who says that the body, when it rises in glory and in power and in incorruptibility, has already become spiritual, it seems absurd and contrary to the meaning of the Apostle to say that it is still entangled in the passions of flesh and blood.

(*On First Principles* 2.10.3)

Origen's emphatic denial of a physical understanding of the resurrection is especially interesting for two reasons.

First, his confidence in the assertion attests the strength of his conviction that such an understanding is "low and mean": the problem is not that physical resurrection is unbelievable, but that the conception is unworthy of the hope that faith speaks of. What Origen's argument presupposes, of course, is that a physical understanding of the resurrection was current in Christian Alexandria. (In Chapter 6, we will see how Christianity came increasingly to value the flesh as a medium of divine vindication.) But he insists, again following Paul's analysis, that the body which is raised in resurrection is continuous with the physical body in principle, but different from it in substance:

So our bodies should be supposed to fall like a grain of wheat into the earth, but implanted in them is the cause that maintains the essence of the body. Although the bodies die and are corrupted and scattered, nevertheless by the word of God that same cause that has all along been safe in the essence of the body raises them up from the earth and restores and refashions them, just as the power that exists in a grain of wheat refashions and restores the grain, after its corruption and death, into a body with stalk and ear. And so in the case of those who shall be counted worthy of obtaining an inheritance in the kingdom of heaven, the cause before mentioned, by which the body is refashioned, at the order of God refashions out of the earthly and animate body a spiritual body, which can dwell in heaven.

(*On First Principles* 2.10.3)

The direction and orientation of Origen's analysis is defined by his concern to describe what in humanity may be regarded as ultimately compatible with the divine. For that reason, physical survival is rejected as an adequate category for explaining the resurrection. Instead, he emphasizes the change of substance that must be involved.

Second, the force behind Origen's assertion is purely dialectical. The resolution of the stated antinomies – "psychic"/"spiritual", "dishonor"/"glory," "corruption"/"incorruption" – involves taking Paul's language as directly applicable to the human condition. In the case of each antinomy, the first item in the pair needs to yield to the spiritual progression of the second item in the pair. That is the progressive logic of Origen's dialectics, now applied comprehensively to human experience. Paul had been comprehensive only in his treatment of Scripture; his application of dialectics outside that realm seems to have been experimental and relatively tentative. The difference between Paul and Origen in the application of progressive dialectics is at first sight subtle, but it proves to have a profound, philosophical impact. As we saw in our discussion of 1 Cor. 15 earlier in this chapter, Paul took some care to build a bridge from the dialectical reading of Scripture to the dialectical reading of human experience. Apostolic tradition, the power of the Spirit in baptism, and the Scriptures of Israel were all deployed to insist upon the truth of the resurrection, and then progressive dialectics could explain the nature of the resurrection. Without question, he opened the possibility that progressive dialectics might be applied generally to human experience, but it was only with Origen that the resulting anthropology and theology was fully articulated.

In Origen's articulation, progressive dialectics insists upon the radical transition which resurrection involves. Although his discussion is a brilliant exegesis of Paul's argument, Origen also elevates the dialectical principle above any other consideration which Paul introduces. What had been in Paul a method for understanding Scripture which was applicable outside that field becomes in Origen the fundamental principle of global spiritual revolution. Only that, in his mind, can do justice to the promise of being raised from the dead.

For all that the transition from flesh to spirit is radical, Origen also makes it clear that personal continuity is involved. To put the matter positively, one is clothed bodily with one's own body, as we have already seen. To put the matter negatively, sins borne by the body of flesh may be thought of as visited upon the body which is raised from the dead:

... just as the saints will receive back the very bodies in which they have lived in holiness and purity during their stay in the habitations of this life, but bright and glorious as a result of the resurrection, so, too, the impious, who in this life have loved the darkness of error and the night of ignorance, will after the resurrection be clothed with murky and black bodies, in order that this very gloom of ignorance, which in the present world has taken possession of the inner parts of their mind, may in the world to come be revealed through the garment of their outward body.

(*On First Principles* 2.10.8)

Although Origen is quite consciously engaging in speculation at this point, he firmly rejects the notion that the flesh is involved in the resurrection, even when biblical promises appear to envisage earthly joys:

Now some men, who reject the labor of thinking and seek after the outward and literal meaning of the law, or rather give way to their own desires and lusts, disciples of the mere letter, consider that the promises of the future are to be looked for in the form of pleasure and bodily luxury. And chiefly on this account they desire after the resurrection to have flesh of such a sort that they will never lack the power to eat and drink and to do all things that pertain to flesh and blood, not following the teaching of the apostle Paul about the resurrection of a "spiritual body."

(*On First Principles* 2.11.2)

His reasons for rejecting such a millenarian view are both exegetical and theological.

Paul is the ground of the apostolic authority he invokes, in a reading we have already seen (1 Cor. 15). He uses that perspective to consider the Scriptures generally (*On First Principles* 2.11.3). But Origen deepens his argument from interpretation with a globally theological one. He maintains that the most urgent longing is the desire "to learn the design of those things which we perceive to have been made by God." This longing is as basic to our minds as light is to the eye: constitutionally, we long for the vision of God (*On First Principles* 2.11.4).

The manner in which Origen develops his own thought is complex, involving a notion of education in paradise prior to one's entry into the realm of heaven proper:

I think that the saints when they depart from this life will remain in some place situated on the earth, which the divine Scripture calls

The implications for understanding Christ are evident, and Augustine does not hesitate to spell them out:

> Even then, when the Lord was born of a virgin . . . it was not the Word of God in his own substance, by which he is equal and co-eternal to the Father . . . but assuredly a creature . . . which could appear to bodily and mortal senses.
>
> (*On the Trinity* III.11)

Here Augustine provides the key to a Christian evaluation of Jesus. He is a mortal person, a "creature" within natural conditions and historical time, and can be understood as such. But just this person also embodies God's "Word," the divine plan for all time. That "Word" was revealed to the prophets of Israel according to their own perception of it, but in the case of Jesus that "Word" – God's own loving design for humanity – actually became flesh. For that reason, all that has been accurately said in the Old Testament may be said to be fulfilled in the New Testament. In his association of Christ with the prophetic Word of God, Augustine reflects a tradition of thought which reaches back to the opening of the Gospel according to John (see John 1:1–18). But he is more acute than most Christian thinkers in his distinction between the created person called Jesus and the eternal Son who is the Father's equal.

God, then, creates as Father and redeems as Son. Likewise, God as Holy Spirit communicates his unique essence; Spirit is God's gift of himself (*On the Trinity* V.11–16). Augustine acknowledges that there is no established vocabulary which can convey the meaning of the Trinity. He is familiar with the reference to "essence" and "nature" among some Greek theologians, to whom we will refer in a moment. He admits that, to refer to what unifies the Trinity, "essence" (*ousia*, in Greek) is better than the common Latin term "substance" (*substantia*; *On the Trinity* V.2–4, see also VII.4–5). His worry about "substance" is that its meaning might be confused with material composition. But whether seen as unique essence or unique substance, Father, Son, and Spirit are to be understood as the exalted Trinity, in which each is God, but there are not three Gods (*On the Trinity* V.8). That is so because they are all aspects of a single and unique essence, the substance of divinity alone.

Augustine's Greek predecessors in the exposition of the Trinity are known as the Cappadocian Fathers (St. Basil, St. Gregory of Nazianzus, St. Gregory of Nyssa), from the region of Asia Minor in which they were active during the fourth century. The Cappadocian

Fathers borrowed from the vocabulary of Greek philosophy in order to explain the relationships among Father, Son, and Spirit. The statement of faith called the Nicene Creed had already established the Son as being "of one substance" (*ousia/substantia*) with the Father, but how could the differences within the Trinity be expressed? The Cappadocians used the term "nature" (*hypostasis*) in Greek; so that they spoke of one essence and three natures. But Augustine, alone with many Latin Christians, complained that the term "nature" seemed pretty much the same as "essence," and in fact both of them could be translated by the Latin term "substance."

For that reason, Augustine accepted the Latin practice of speaking of the Trinity as three "persons" in one "substance," rather than of three "natures" in one "essence." But he warned his readers that the words used have no authority in themselves; we only use them "in order that we might not be obliged to remain silent" (*On the Trinity* V.9). Despite such warnings, however, different uses of language to explore the Trinity have caused a deep rift between what came to be called the Orthodox Church in the East and what came to be called the Catholic Church in the West.

Knowledge of the Trinity must obviously be beyond words, because words emerge from the terms and relations of this world, not directly from God. When Augustine turned to explore the true nature of God, he found that the best possible medium would be to analyze love. After all, God is love (so 1 John 4:7–10) and God commands love (so Mark 12:28–34 and parallels); it must be that love is the gift of God within us, so we must understand love in order to know God. In general terms, we can even say that the Trinity is reflected in the relationship between the lover, the beloved, and love itself (*On the Trinity* VIII.7–IX.2).

Augustine's emphasis on the interior gift of love led him to turn away from exterior relations among people (which the Cappadocian Fathers had in any case explored) and to seek the truth of love within the mind. There, his favorite analogy to the Trinity was that a mind is possessed of memory, understanding, and will, and these are not "three minds, but one mind" (*On the Trinity* X.11–12): "For I remember that I have memory, understanding, and will; and I understand that I understand, will, and remember; and I will that I will, remember, and understand. . . ." Augustine's analogy of a single human mind has led to the accusation that the differences among the Trinity are minimized. On the other hand, the Cappadocians' analogy of three people living in a village had led to the accusation that their picture of the Trinity was practically of three Gods. In the climate of controversy during the fourth and fifth centuries, it is doubtful that *any* analogy of the Trinity, no matter how nuanced, could have avoided causing offense in some quarter or another.

But the fundamental insight which animates the work of the Cappadocians and Augustine alike is that the one God is known to us in three aspects, and that God is related to himself in those aspects. The Trinity is not just a way of knowing God, but an account of how God is. His creativity, his redemption, his communication of himself, are all essential and distinct aspects of his being God.

The key to an understanding of the Trinity, and of its success as a teaching within Christianity, is found in its joint explanation of our experience of God *and* of the relations within God. Christian baptismal experience of Father, Son, and Spirit (see Matt. 28:16–20) stood in an apparent antinomy to the declaration of the Old Testament of God's oneness (see Exod. 20:3; Deut. 6:4–5). In that both Scripture and experience of the Spirit were accepted as sources of revelation, resolving that antinomy was more than a matter of intellectual integrity. The integrity of revelation itself was at stake.

One attempt at a resolution is known as modalism:[3] reference was made to various modes of our access to God. One problem with that attempt was that it apparently reduced the possibility of knowing God to the exclusion of many other different modalities, such as prophecy and angelic mediation within Israel, and the philosophical insight of teachers such as Plato outside of Israel. Origen was committed to interpret the divine nature in a way that explained the diversity of revelation, without betraying the Old Testament's resistance to polytheism. The option of polytheism was not even seriously considered by Origen, because for him – as for the vast majority of Graeco-Roman thought during his time – polytheism was both implausible and gave license to self-indulgence. Religious and moral thinkers in Late Antiquity recognized that the gods of Greece and Rome looked too much like the interests and passions of those who made them to amount to a serious account of divinity.

Origen, then, faced two antinomies at once, and both concerned the divine nature. The first antinomy was the classical Christian dichotomy between baptismal experience and the Old Testament's monotheism. The second antinomy was the Hellenistic paradox that polytheistic religious traditions contradicted the philosophical conviction of a divine unity at the base of the world. Origen applied his progressive dialectics to both antinomies at once, and the result was a normative understanding of the Trinity. Augustine, also from the Platonic tradition within Christianity, was able to meditate as lucidly as he did on the divine nature because the dialectical resolution of the two great antinomies of Hellenistic Christianity had already been resolved by Origen.

Origen understood the Father as God unconditioned, unapproachable by mind and uncontained by being (*On First Principles* 1.1.6). But even as God is unconditioned, and his complete transcendence is an essential quality of the divine nature, it is also the case that God as God creates beings other than himself. In that creation, God's image – his Son – becomes the point of generation for the multiplicity of divine aspects of which people may become aware, and which are the source of human life and of all being (*On First Principles* 1.2.3–4).

The precise point at which Origen exercises his progressive dialectics is in his explanation of the relationship between the Father and the Son. He boldly and famously asserted that there was no time when the Son did not exist (*On First Principles* 1.2.4). That is, although the Father begets the Son, that begetting is an eternal act. The Father has a distinct nature, namely divine transcendence; and the Son has a distinct nature, namely the mediation of transcendence so as to create the world. But the Son is not dependent on the world; he exists from eternity as of the divine essence. And the dialectical truth of God's essence is that it is both transcendent and creative, Father and Son.

Finally, Origen's picture of the distinct "natures" (*hypostases*) of God within a single "essence" (*ousia*) is filled out with his understanding of the Spirit. The Father and the Son are internal aspects of God, and on that basis explain how God may be addressed in those different ways. But that interior diversity also requires a knowledge of itself in the act of creation. That self-awareness and self-realization of God is just what Origen calls Spirit (see *On First Principles* 1.3.1–4 and *Commentary on John* 2.10.75). His Trinity, developed with the inherited language of Father, Son, and Spirit, is in fact a dialectical exploration of the essence of God. God is described as naturally transcendent, naturally creative, naturally self-aware.

These three complementary natures make up a single essence in a way which resolves the classical Christian dichotomy between a single God and the divinity of Jesus with the Spirit. Moreover, the status of the Son as the eternally begotten image of the eternally begetting Father permits the Son to be the meeting-place of the many, many aspects of God in the world which have been known and which will be known. On Origen's account of the Trinity, Plato and Hesiod may be understood as revelatory. For that reason, Origen's Trinity is a contribution to Hellenistic philosophy and religion, as well as to Christianity. Both contributions are possible because Origen applied progressive dialectics, not only to an understanding of Scripture, faith, and humanity, but also as an analytic tool for meditative dissection of the natures of God.

PART II

SEEKING TRUTH
The Character of
the Arguments

5

ARGUMENTS FROM NATURAL HISTORY IN THE MISHNAH AND IN LEVITICUS RABBAH

To settle disputes, arguments of one of three types would serve in Rabbinic Judaism. Can we specify the rules of argument and their types? First comes the argument from authority. Specifically, a sage might invoke for the case at hand the authority of Heaven (also known as, God in the Torah) or of Heaven mediated by surrogates on earth (sage, priest, king). Evidence on behalf of a given proposition and against its opposite would then derive from Scripture as interpreted by sages, and a valid argument would consist in citing a verse of Scripture and showing how the wording or substance of the verse settled matters.

Second, one might set forth an array of evidence deriving from the nature of facts that are acknowledged by all parties to the dispute. These facts might derive from the social order, the everyday world of nature, or from Scripture. The facts would then be alleged to speak for themselves, for example, these facts bear implications for our case, or they prove the opposite of the case of the other party. Precisely how that argument is worked out will occupy us in this chapter and its companion.

Third, one might make a case based on probative events also deriving from Scripture, paradigmatic events that establish a pattern to make sense of otherwise random happenings. Chapters 7 and 8 show how, for Judaism and Christianity, paradigmatic reading of historical events served to prove propositions.

The one argument we never find appeals to God's direct intervention in favor of one view and against another ("if God takes that view, it must be the correct one" being the supposititious argument). Supernatural intrusion contradicts the basic premises of reason as sages understand the rationality of the universe. God's intrusion into human discourse, except on the same terms that govern sages themselves, indeed, is explicitly rejected in favor of sages' own modes of composing arguments, the following story forming the *locus classicus* for the matter:

[1.A] *There we have learned:* **If one cut [a clay oven] into parts and put sand between the parts,**

[B] **R. Eliezer declares the oven broken-down and therefore insusceptible to uncleanness.**

[C] **And sages declare it susceptible.**

[D] **And this is what is meant by the oven of Akhnai [M. Kel. 5:10].**

[E] *Why* [is it called] the oven of Akhnai?

[F] Said R. Judah said Samuel, "It is because they surrounded it with argument as with a snake and proved it was insusceptible to uncleanness."

2 [A] *It has been taught on Tannaite authority:*

[B] On that day R. Eliezer produced all of the arguments in the world, but they did not accept them from him. So he said to them, "If the law accords with my position, this carob tree will prove it."

[C] The carob was uprooted from its place by a hundred cubits – and some say, four hundred cubits.

[D] They said to him, "There is no proof from a carob tree."

[E] So he went and said to them, "If the law accords with my position, let the stream of water prove it."

[F] The stream of water reversed flow.

[G] They said to him, "There is no proof from a stream of water."

[H] So he went and said to them, "If the law accords with my position, let the walls of the school house prove it."

[I] The walls of the school house tilted toward falling.

[J] Joshua rebuked them, saying to them, "If disciples of sages are contending with one another in matters of law, what business do you have?"

[K] They did not fall on account of the honor owing to R. Joshua, but they also did not straighten up on account of the honor owing to R. Eliezer, and to this day they are still tilted.

[L] So he went and said to them, "If the law accords with my position, let the Heaven prove it!"

[M] An echo came forth, saying, "What business have you with R. Eliezer, for the law accords with his position under all circumstances!"

[N]   Joshua stood up on his feet and said, "'It is not in heaven'
       (Dt. 30:12)."

[O]   *What is the sense of,* "'It is not in heaven' (Dt. 30:12)"*?*

[P]   Said R. Jeremiah, "[The sense of Joshua's statement is this]:
       For the Torah has already been given from Mount Sinai, so
       we do not pay attention to echoes, since you have already
       written in the Torah at Mount Sinai, 'After the majority you
       are to incline' (Ex. 23:2)."

[Q]   *Nathan came upon Elijah and said to him, "What did the
       Holy One, blessed be he, do at that moment?"*

[R]   *He said to him, "He laughed and said, 'My children have over-
       come me, my children have overcome me!'"*

(Babylonian Talmud Baba Mesia 59A–B)

Before us is one of the most famous and representative passages of the
Talmud, the claim that human beings may argue with God – and
win! God is bound by the same logic that governs our minds, and we
by that that governs God's. Through the ages, those concluding words
have inspired the disciples of sages at their work: through intelligent
argument the sage may overcome in argument the very Creator of
heaven and earth, the One who gives the Torah – and is bound by its
rules too. Here, in the Torah, humanity is not only like God but, in
context, equal to God because subject to the same logic. In secular
terms the conception of theoretical mathematics as the actual description of nature corresponds. The one argument we never find in the
Rabbinic canon appeals to Heaven for validation.

If logic governs both God and the sages, then what about evidence
and argumentation from evidence? Here the second and third types
of arguments enter, those that appeal to the nature of things, those
that invoke paradigmatic structures to impart order and meaning –
therefore probative weight – to events formed into an intelligible
pattern. The former type of argument concerns us here and in the following chapter, the latter in the concluding two chapters.

One powerful argument for a given proposition, and against its
opposite, derives from the demonstration out of established facts,
accepted by all parties, that said proposition simply states what is so.
If, therefore, one party to a dispute can prove that the other has his
facts wrong, the issue is resolved, the argument being decisive. When
it comes to identifying the argument in the Rabbinic literature the
facts speak for themselves. We turn to an entire document for our
case, that is, the Mishnah, which systematically arrays established

facts through a system of classification by indicative traits, on the one side, and hierarchization in the setting of classification, on the other. Indicative traits for their part may derive from any source acknowledged by all parties, whether Scripture or established practice; the main point is the work of classification and hierarchization. A single example suffices to show the implicit argument that takes place in the correct display of acknowledged facts. The conflict concerns the status of the king and the high priest: which is the higher? The argument then lays out the facts of the matter pertaining to each, and that argument settles the issue.

In the following composition, the king and the high priest are set forth in such a way that the rights and immunities of each are compared to those assigned to the other. By consequence, the high priest is shown to be a subordinate figure, the king an autocephalous authority. If we work through the comparison's terms, it introduces us to the power and authority of both the king and the high priest. So let us consider the entire passage here. The comparison runs as follows:

A A high priest (1) judges, and [others] judge him;

B (2) gives testimony, and [others] give testimony about him;

C (3) performs the rite of removing the shoe with his wife.

D (4) [Others] enter levirate marriage with his wife, but he does not enter into levirate marriage,

E because he is prohibited to marry a widow.

F (5) [If] he suffers a death [in his family], he does not follow the bier.

G "But when [the bearers of the bier] are not visible, he is visible; when they are visible, he is not.

H "And he goes with them to the city gate," the words of R. Meir.

I R. Judah says, "He never leaves the sanctuary,

J "since it says, '*Nor shall he go out of the sanctuary*' (Lev. 21:12)."

K And hen he givers comfort to others

L the accepted practice is for all the people to pass on after another, and the appointed [prefect of the priests] stands between him and the people.

M And when he receives consolation from others,

N all the people say to him, "Let us be your atonement."

O And he says to them, "May you blesses by Heaven."

P (6) and when they provide him with the funeral meal,

Q all the people sit on the ground, while he sits on a stool.

M. 2:1

A (1) The king does not judge, and [others] do not judge him;

B (2) does not give testimony, and [others] do not give testimony about him;

C (3) does not perform the rite of removing the shoe, and others do not perform the rite of removing the shoe with his wife;

D (4) does not enter into Levirate marriage, nor [do his brothers] enter levirate marriage with his wife.

E R. Judah says, "If he wanted to perform the rite of removing the show or to enter into levirate marriage, his memory is a blessing."

F They said to him, "They pay no attention to him [if he expressed the wish to do so.]"

G [Others] do not marry his widow.

H R. Judah says, "A king may marry the widow of a king.

I For so we find in the case of David, that he marries the widow of Saul.

J For it is said, *And I gave you your master's house and your master's wives into your embrace* (II Sam. 12:8)."

M. 2:2

A (5) [If] he suffers a death in his family, he does not leave the gate of his palace.

B R. Judah says, "If he wants to go out after the bier, he goes out,

C "for thus we find in the case of David, that he went out after the bier of Abner,

D since it is said, '*And King David followed the bier*' (II Sam. 3:31)."

E They said to him, "This action was only to appease the people."

F (6) And when they provide him with the funeral meal, all the people sit on the ground, while he sits on a couch.

M. 2:3
(M. Sanhedrin 2:1–3)

The conflict between king and high priest is now resolved by the argument from classification of acknowledged facts. What we see is an exercise in classification – comparison and contrast of two offices of the same category – and hierarchization. The passage's contrast stands clear: by reason of his genealogy, the high priest enjoys certain immunities in his person; the king, who exercises power above the community, stands immune from all rules that apply to the community. The two heads of state therefore are alike, but different – and the king is the superior figure. The high priest and the king form a single genus, but two distinct species, and the variations between the species form a single set of taxonomic indicators. The one is like the other in these ways, unlike the other in those ways.[1]

It suffices to state that nearly the entire Mishnah is comprised of arguments formed in precisely the same way: lists of facts so constituted as to yield arguments on behalf of one proposition and against its opposite. And the case at hand shows us nothing other than a standard syllogism. By syllogism is meant "discourse in which, certain things being stated, something other than what is stated follows of necessity from their being so."[2] When we establish the general truths concerning the high priest and the king, we identify a third truth, concerning the priority of the latter over the former, and that truth is one of deduction.

While the Mishnah may be properly read as philosophy formed out of arguments set forth through lists and the hierarchization of the things that are listed, the document certainly does not make abstract philosophical points or ordinarily express its principles in explicit generalizations. All points concerning classification, for example, are made through talk of pots and pans, of menstruation and dead creeping things, of ordinary water which, because of the circumstance of its collection and location, possesses extraordinary power. The compositions of the Mishnah speak of the commonplace corpse and ubiquitous diseased person; of genitalia and excrement, toilet seats and the flux of penises, of stems of pomegranates and stalks of leeks; of rain and earth; of wood, metal, glass and hide. And these are treated not as symbols or even as examples but are made to carry the full weight of discourse. I cannot imagine less fertile ground for the seed of abstract theorizing on the nature of things.

The Mishnah therefore provides an extreme example of how practical logic and applied reason come to expression and are worked out solely through the nitty-gritty of ordinary and everyday life. Its mode of speech – the way it speaks, not only what it says – is testimony to its conception that within the everyday are contained the highest and most abstract truths not merely of wisdom but of knowledge, in our language, natural philosophy or science.[3] If things are orderly, then out of the chaos of the here and now, we must show it. Just as in contemporary empirical, experimental science the case stands for the principle, so in the Mishnah, the cases bear the entire burden of analytical and principled thought. Sages set forth a philosophy of classification, aimed at demonstrating the unity of all being: many things are one thing, and one thing contains many things. The Mishnah's sages' modes of thought, focused upon the correct classification of things, sustained a program of thought concerned with what was classified. And at issue was, as I said, when many things were really one thing (the many and the one, the species and the genus), and when one thing was really many things (the one and the many, the genus and the species). The problems of thought took up the mixture of distinct things, each subject to its own taxic indicators, and how several grids of classification, interposed upon one another in such a mixture, were to be sorted out. These theoretical issues can have come to practical expression in the analysis of the nature of things, for example, biology or ethnology. But in the Mishnah they concerned the account of things that Scripture provided. It was revelation, not nature, that defined the data for classification and reclassification. But it was philosophy, not tradition, that defined the method and therefore determined the propositions. That interest more than any other defines the exegetical program of the Mishnah and marks it as philosophical.

One problem of classification concerns the issue of being and becoming, when an object ceases to be what it has been and becomes something else, that is, leaves its prior classification and enters a new one. To understand what follows we have to know that there are different types of cultic uncleanness that affect different sorts of objects. If an object may be used for lying or sitting, it is susceptible to pressure-uncleanness (midras-uncleanness). That is a most severe kind of uncleanness. If it may be used for a receptacle (but not for lying or sitting) it is susceptible to corpse-uncleanness. What if an object served for lying or sitting but was broken and now serves as a receptacle? Then the uncleanness affecting it by reason of its former classification no longer applies, but a different uncleanness does pertain. And what happens if we change the status of an object, for example, dismantle a bed? At what point does the definition of the bed shift? And, when it shifts, what is the status or classification of the parts and of the remnant of the whole? These are problems of mixture too, but different mixture altogether from the foregoing.

[18:5 A]   [As to] a bed which was unclean with midras-uncleanness –

[B]   [if] a short side and two legs are removed,

[C]   it [still] is unclean.

[D]   [If] the long side and two legs [are removed],

[E]   [it] is clean.

[F]   R. Nehemiah declares unclean.

[G]   [If] one cut off two tongues at diagonally opposite cor-
        ners, [or] cut off two legs at diagonally opposite corners
        by a square handbreadth, or diminished it [to] less than a
        handbreadth,

[H]   [it] is clean.

[18:6 A] [As to] a bed which was unclean with midras-unclean-
        ness —

[B]   [if] a long [side] was broken, and then repaired it,

[C]   [the bed still is] unclean with midras-uncleanness.

[D]   [If] a second was broken, and one repaired it, it [the bed
        as a whole] is clean from midras-uncleanness but unclean
        with the uncleanness imparted by contact with midras-
        uncleanness.

[E]   [If] one did not have time to repair the first before the
        second was broken, it [the bed] is clean.

                                (Mishnah-Tractate Kelim 18:5–6)

Now the question of classification need not be expressed in terms of
mixtures, e.g., a combination of two or more classifications that apply
to a single thing. The theoretical issue may also be expressed in terms
of classification of objects, and all issues of classification turn out to
reframe the question of mixture, as we shall now see.

Here we ask, when does an object entirely lose its primary character through the breakage and replacement of its principal parts, so as
to constitute a fundamentally new utensil? If one replaces the eight
parts of a bed, for example, at what point do the new parts form an
essentially new bed, rather than the old one? Is it when we have put
in five new parts in place of the original ones? What other criteria can
we establish? M.Kel. 18:5–6 (continued at 7–9) give the answer, and
it is a fundamental conception of classification indeed. When those
parts that give the original utensil its intrinsic character, by carrying
out its primary function, have been replaced by new ones, what happens? Even though the original utensil is superficially the same and in
being, the utensil before us has ceased to exhibit its original character.
It is adjudged a new utensil; the old utensil is as if it were broken. Yet
another example works its way through the same problem:

[18:7 A] [As to] a bed leg which was unclean with midras-unclean-
        ness and [which] one attached to the bed —

[B]   the whole [bed] is unclean with midras-uncleanness.

[C]   [If] one took it off, it [the leg] is unclean with midras-uncleanness, and the bed [is unclean] with the uncleanness imparted by contact with midras-uncleanness.

[D]   [If] it was unclean with seven-day uncleanness and one attached it to the bed, the whole thing is unclean with the seven-day uncleanness.

[E]   [If] one took it off, it is unclean with seven-day uncleanness, and the bed is unclean with uncleanness which lasts until the evening.

[F]   [If] it was unclean with the uncleanness which lasts until the evening, and one attached it to the bed, the whole thing is unclean with the uncleanness that lasts until the evening.

[G]   [If] one removed it, it is unclean with the uncleanness that lasts until the evening, and the bed is clean.

[H]   And so with the tooth of the plough.

(Mishnah-Tractate Kelm 18:7)

This issue is spelled out through removes of uncleanness, and that makes sense, since we wish to express gradations of classification (which is to say, mixtures in a mode different from that we observed at Mishnah-tractate Tohorot), not a complete shift from one to another classification (that is, merely unclean to merely clean). These removes in the problem that follows now are three: midras-uncleanness, the most severe, a Father of uncleanness; contact with midras-uncleanness, unclean at the first remove, a less severe degree; and entirely clean. These gradations express the classifications as follows: the former bed is intact; the old bed is no longer intact but does not yet constitute a wholly new one; and the bed is entirely new. I cannot imagine a more brilliant way of translating abstract principles into concrete and homely ones.

[19:7 A] A box whose opening is on top is susceptible to corpse-uncleanness.

[B]   [If, after contracting corpse-uncleanness] it was damaged on the top, it [still] is unclean with corpse-uncleanness.

[C]   [If] it was damaged on the bottom, it is clean.

[D]   The drawers which are in it are unclean and are not connected to it.

[19:8 A] The shepherd's bag, the inner pocket of which was broken, is unclean, and it [the bag] is not connected to it [the pocket].

[B]   The goatskin, of which the testicle bags contain with it, and [the testicle bags of which] were damaged –

[C]   [the bags] are clean,

[D]   for they do not hold [water] in their normal fashion.

[19:9 A] A box which was damaged on its side is susceptible both to midras-uncleanness and to corpse-uncleanness.

[B]   Said R. Yosé, "When? When it is not ten handbreadths high, or when it does not have a rim a handbreadth high."

[C]   If it was damaged on the top, it is susceptible to corpse-uncleanness.

[D]   [If] it was damaged on the bottom,

[E]   R. Meir declares unclean.

[F]   And sages declare clean, because [if] the primary purpose is annulled, the secondary purpose is annulled.

(Mishnah-Tractate Kelim 19:7–10)

Classification-rules guide us to the problem of definition. That problem is worked out in a variety of ways. To show how we classify by determining how we define an object, I give yet another set of cases. These cases build upon the foregoing and cannot have been set forth without the rules (not philosophical principles) explained in the items just given. Now M.Kel. 19:7–9 take up wooden boxes and their susceptibility to uncleannesses of various removes. If they can be used for two purposes, they will be susceptible to uncleanness under two distinct counts, if for only one purpose, then only for one count. Thus if a box can be used for both storage and sitting, according to M.19:7ff., it is susceptible to both corpse- and midras-uncleanness. What if a box is not fit for storage but remains fit for sitting? Will it be susceptible to midras-uncleanness?

The problem of how we define or classify is exemplified, but the problem is abstract, not merely a rule deriving from a case, but a principle that applies to entire areas of thought. The issue is: do we take account of secondary uses or functions of a utensil when the primary purpose is no longer served? One authority maintains that if a utensil is not useful for one thing, it is still useful for some other and remains susceptible to the uncleanness pertinent to that other use. A utensil is not defined solely in terms of its primary function. Although the maker clearly intended to use the object for that primary function, his intention has not defined the character of the object; its function defines the character and use. The other authority maintains that once the primary function of a utensil is no longer served, the secondary functions are treated as of no account. If the owner did not intend the utensil for a specific purpose, then the utensil is not regarded as whole and complete and it will be clean. The issue of classification again depends upon whether or not we admit the consideration of initial purpose.

So much for the Mishnah's mode of argument through a process of analysis of the traits of things. But what of Scripture's contribution? Any account of the character of arguments deemed probative by Rabbinic Judaism must focus on the uses of Scripture in the context of conflict. That is especially critical when we recall that, in the canonical writings of this Judaism, Scripture took a subordinated role defining the structure of documents only occasionally, and then in competition with the Mishnah. The principal writings – the Tosefta and two huge Talmuds – organize themselves around the Mishnah. Some theological compilations, such as Pesiqta deRab Kahana, invoke Scripture only for proof-texts but do not take shape around Scripture. Still others treat Scripture as a pretext for setting forth free-standing propositions, entering into the inner exegetical life of Scripture only in order to make a point sustained by, but not critical to, Scripture itself. The place of Scripture in the world of probative argument is therefore not to be gainsaid but rather identified and instantiated.

For that purpose one of the canon's greatest theological exercises – a compilation of demonstrations of important propositions, therefore refutations of contrary propositions, through a sequence of thirty seven massive exercises – will serve to characterize modes of argument that invoke shared facts of the natural or social worlds as Scripture preserves those facts. It is Leviticus Rabbah, generally assigned to the mid-fifth century, about a generation beyond the closure of the Talmud of the Land of Israel in c. 400 CE. In that document Scripture proves paramount on the surface, but subordinated in the deep structure of the logic of Leviticus Rabbah. Why so? Because Scripture enjoys no autonomous standing, for example, as the sole source of facts. It does not dictate the order of discussion. It does not (by itself) determine the topics to be taken up, since its verses, cited one by one in sequence, do not tell us how matters will proceed. Scripture, moreover, does not allow us to predict what proposition a given set of verses will yield. On the contrary, because of the insistence that one verse be read in light of another, one theme in light of another, augmentative one, Leviticus Rabbah prohibits us from predicting at the outset, merely by reading a given verse of Scripture, the way in which a given theme will be worked out or the way in which a given proposition will impart a message through said theme.

So, in all, the order of Scripture does not govern the sequence of discourse, the themes of Scripture do not tell us what themes will be taken up, the propositions of Scripture about its stated themes (what Scripture says, in its context, about a given topic) do not define the propositions of Leviticus Rabbah in regard to that topic. The upshot is simple. Scripture contributes everything and nothing. It provides the decoration, the facts, much language. The editors, doing the work of selection, making their points through juxtaposition of things not otherwise brought into contact with one another, are the ones who compose the arguments on behalf of the propositions they themselves have framed.

If, moreover, Scripture contributes facts, so too do the ones who state those ineluctable truths that are expressed in parables, and so too do the ones who tell stories, also exemplifying truths, about great heroes and villains. No less, of course, but, in standing, also no more than these, Scripture makes its contribution along with other sources of social truth. Greek science focused upon physics. Then the laws of Israel's salvation serve as the physics of the sages. But Greek science derived facts and built theorems on the basis of other sources besides physics; the philosophers also, after all, studied ethnography, ethics, politics, and history. For the sages at hand, along these same lines, parables, exemplary tales, and completed paragraphs of thought deriving from other sources (not to exclude the Mishnah, Tosefta, Sifra, Genesis Rabbah and such literary compositions that had been made ready for the Talmud of the Land of Israel), these too make their contribution of data subject to analysis. All of these sources of not truth but true facts, together, were directed toward the discovery of philosophical laws for the understanding of Israel's life now, and in the age to come.

How do sages read Scripture the way philosophers read nature? Here are the key traits. They yield:

1 Scripture, for one thing, forms a timeless present, with the affairs of the present day read back into the past and the past into the present, with singular events absorbed into Scripture's paradigms.

2 Scripture is read whole and atomistically. Everything speaks to everything else, but only one thing speaks at a time.

3 Scripture is read as an account of a seamless world, encompassing

present and past alike, and Scripture is read atemporally and ahistorically.

How in context is the corpus of facts received and read?

1 Scripture is read whole, because the framers pursue issues of thought that demand all data pertain to all times and all contexts. The authors are philosophers, looking for rules and their verification. Scripture tells stories, to be sure. But these exemplify facts of social life and national destiny: the laws of Israel's life.

2 Scripture is read atomistically, because each of its components constitutes a social fact, ever relevant to the society of which it forms a part, with that society everywhere uniform.

3 Scripture is read as a source of facts pertinent to historical and contemporary issues alike, because the issues at hand when worked out will indicate the prevailing laws, the rules that apply everywhere, all the time, to everyone of Israel.

Accordingly, there is no way for Scripture to be read except as a source of facts about that ongoing reality that forms the focus and the center of discourse, the life of the unique social entity, Israel. But the simple logic conveyed by the parable also contributes its offering of facts. The simple truth conveyed by the tale of the great man, the exemplary event of the rabbinic sage, the memorable miracle – these too serve as well as facts of Scripture. The several truths therefore stand alongside and at the same level as the truths of Scripture, which is not the sole source of rules or cases. The facts of Scripture stand no higher than those of the parable, on the one side, or of the tale of the sage, on the other. Why not? Because to philosophers and scientists, facts are facts, whatever their origin or point of application.

What we have in Leviticus Rabbah, therefore, is the result of the mode of thought and argument (the two are indistinguishable) not of prophets or historians, but of philosophers and scientists. The framers propose not to lay down, but to discover, rules governing Israel's life. As we find the rules of nature by identifying and classifying facts of natural life, so we find rules of society by identifying and classifying the facts of Israel's social life. In both modes of inquiry we make sense of things by bringing together like specimens and finding out whether they form a species, then bringing together like species and finding out whether they form a genus – in all, classifying data and identifying the rules that make possible the classification.

That sort of thinking has already established its presence for us in the Mishnah, for it lies at the deepest level of list-making, which is, as I said, a work of offering a proposition and facts (for social rules) as much as a genus and its species (for rules of nature). Once discovered, the social rules of Israel's national life of course yield explicit statements, such as that God hates the arrogant and loves the humble. The readily-assembled syllogism follows: if one is arrogant, God will hate him, and if he is humble, God will love him. The logical status of these statements is, in context, as secure and unassailable as the logical status of statements about physics, ethics, or politics, as these emerge in philosophical thought. What differentiates the statements is not their logical status – as sound, scientific philosophy – but only their subject-matter, on the one side, and distinctive rhetoric, on the other.

The heart of the matter lies in laying forth the rules of life – of Israel's life and salvation. These rules derive from the facts of history, as much as the rules of the Mishnah derive from the facts of society (and, in context, the rules of philosophy derive from the facts of nature). Scripture then never stands all by itself. Its exalted position at the center of all discourse proves contingent, never absolute. It contributes facts to help form arguments on behalf of free-standing propositions, just as does nature, common sense (parables), sagacity (tales of sages' exemplary conduct), and the like. The authors of the document's compositions make generalizations which are free-standing. They express cogent propositions through extended compositions, not episodic ideas. Earlier, things people wished to say were attached to predefined statements based on an existing text, constructed in accord with an organizing logic independent of the systematic expression of a single, well-framed idea. Now the authors so collect and arrange their materials that an abstract proposition emerges. Argumentation for that proposition is not expressed only or mainly through episodic restatements assigned, as I said, to an order established by a base-text. Rather it emerges through a logic of its own, a logic that appeals to the self-evidently probative weight of established facts.

What is new is the move from an essentially exegetical mode of logical discourse to a fundamentally philosophical one. It is the shift from discourse framed around an established (hence old) text to syllogistic argument organized around a proposed (hence new) theorem or proposition. What changes, therefore, is the way in which cogent thought takes place, as people move from discourse contingent on some prior principle of organization to discourse autonomous of a ready-made program inherited from an earlier paradigm. Accordingly, when we listen to the framers of Leviticus Rabbah, we see how statements in the document at hand thus become intelligible not contingently, that is, on the strength of an established text, but *a priori*, that is, on the basis of a deeper logic of meaning and an independent principle of rhetorical intelligibility. Leviticus Rabbah is topical, not exegetical. Each of its thirty-seven parashiyyot pursues its given topic and develops points relevant to that topic. It is logical, in that (to repeat) discourse appeals to an underlying principle of composition and intelligibility, and that logic inheres in the facts adduced in evidence. Logic is what joins one sentence to the next and forms the whole into paragraphs of meaning, intelligible propositions, each with its place and sense in a still larger, accessible system. Because of logic one mind connects to another, public discourse becomes possible, debate on issues of general intelligibility takes place, and an anthology of statements about a single subject becomes a composition of theorems about that subject. The argument in Leviticus Rabbah (and not only there) consists in an exercise in analogical thinking – something is like something else, stands for, evokes, or symbolizes that which is quite outside itself. It may be the opposite of something else, in which case it conforms to the exact opposite of the rules that govern that something else. The reasoning is analogical or it is contrastive, and the fundamental logic is taxonomic.

In light of the account of the syllogistic possibilities at hand, we may identify the theorems of argumentation operative in our document (and not here alone, of course). What is important is that the logic at hand proves subject to verification on grounds other than those supplied by the proof-texts alone. How so? The appeal is to an autonomous realm, namely, reason confirmed by experience. The repeated claim is not that things are so merely because Scripture says what it says, but that things happened as they happened in accord with laws we may verify or test (as Scripture, among other sources of facts, tells us). The emphasis is on the sequence of events, the interrelationship exhibited by them. How does Scripture in particular participate? It is not in particular at all. Scripture serves as a source of information, much as any history of the world or of a nation would provide sources of information: facts. Who makes use of these facts? In our own time it is the social scientist, seeking the rules that social entities are supposed to exhibit. In the period at hand it was the rabbinical philosopher, seeking the rules governing Israel's life. So far as people seek rules and regularities, the search is one of logic, of philosophy. It follows that our document rests upon logical argumentation. Its framers, rabbis, served as philosophers in the ancient meaning of the term. And, in consequence, Scripture for its part is transformed into the source of those facts that supply both the problem, chaos, and the solution, order, rule, organized in lists. So Scripture in the hands of the rabbis of our document corresponds to nature in the hands of the great Greek philosophers.

The Mishnah makes its principal points by collecting three or five examples of a given rule. The basic rule is not stated, but it is exemplified through the several statements of its application. The reader may then infer the generalization from its specific exemplifications. Sometimes, but not often, the generalization will be made explicit. The whole then constitutes an exercise in rhetoric and logic carried out through list-making. And the same is true in Leviticus Rabbah. But it makes lists of different things from those of the Mishnah: events, not everyday situations. The framers of Leviticus Rabbah revert to sequences of events, all of them exhibiting the same definitive traits and the same ultimate results, for example, arrogance, downfall, not one time but many; humility, salvation, over and over again, and so throughout. Indeed, if I had to select a single paramount trait of argument in Leviticus Rabbah, it would be the theorem stated by the making of a list of similar examples. The search for the rules lies through numerous instances that, all together, yield the besought rule.

In context, therefore, we have in the thirty-seven parashiyyot of Leviticus Rabbah the counterpart to the list-making that defined the labor of the philosophers of the Mishnah. Through composing lists of items joined by a monothetic definitive trait, the framers produce underlying or overriding rules always applicable. Here too, through lists of facts of history, the foundations of social life rise to the surface. All of this, we see, constitutes a species of a molecular argument, framed in very definite terms, for example, Nebuchadnezzar, Sennacherib, David, Josiah did so-and-so with such-and-such a result. So, as I said, the mode of argument at hand is the assembly of instances of a common law. The argument derives from the proper construction of a statement of that law in something close to a syllogism. The syllogistic statement often, though not invariably, occurs at the outset, all instances of so-and-so produce such-and-such a result, followed by the required catalogue.

To show in concrete terms how Leviticus Rabbah proves its points and so formulates its arguments, we take the proposition that God favors the pursued over the pursuer.

[1A] "God seeks what has been driven away" (Qoh. 3:15).

[B] R. Huna in the name of R. Joseph said, "It is always the case that 'God seeks what has been driven away' [favoring the victim].

[C] You find when a righteous man pursues a righteous man, 'God seeks what has been driven away.'

[D] When a wicked man pursues a wicked man, 'God seeks what has been driven away.'

[E] All the more so when a wicked man pursues a righteous man, 'God seeks what has been driven away.'

[F] [The same principle applies] even when you come around to a case in which a righteous man pursues a wicked man, 'God seeks what has been driven away.'"

[2A] R. Yosé b. R. Yudan in the name of R. Yosé b. R. Nehorai says, "It is always the case that the Holy One, blessed be he, demands an accounting for the blood of those who have been pursued from the hand of the pursuer.

[B] Abel was pursued by Cain, and God sought [an accounting for] the pursued: 'And the Lord looked [favorably] upon Abel and his meal offering' [Gen. 4:4].

[C] Noah was pursued by his generation, and God sought [an accounting for] the pursued: 'You and all your household shall come into the ark' [Gen. 7:1]. And it says, 'For this is like the days of Noah to me, as I swore [that the waters of Noah should no more go over the earth]' [Is. 54:9].

[D] Abraham was pursued by Nimrod, 'and God seeks what has been driven away': 'You are the Lord, the God who chose Abram and brought him out of Ur' [Neh. 9:7].

[E] Isaac was pursued by Ishmael, 'and God seeks what has been driven away': 'For through Isaac will seed be called for you' [Gen. 21:12].

[F] Jacob was pursued by Esau, 'and God seeks what has been driven away': 'For the Lord has chosen Jacob, Israel for his prized possession' [Ps. 135:4].

[G] Moses was pursued by Pharaoh, 'and God seeks what has been driven away': 'Had not Moses His chosen stood in the breach before Him' [Ps. 106:23].

[H] David was pursued by Saul, 'and God seeks what has been driven away': 'And he chose David, his servant' [Ps. 78:70].

[I]   Israel was pursued by the nations, 'and God seeks what has been driven away': 'And you has the Lord chosen to be a people to him' [Deut. 14:2].

[J]   And the rule applies also to the matter of offerings. A bull is pursued by a lion, a sheep is pursued by a wolf, a goat is pursued by a leopard.

[K]   Therefore the Holy One, blessed be he, has said, 'Do not make offerings before me from those animals that pursue, but from those that are pursued: 'When a bull, a sheep, or a goat is born'".

(Leviticus Rabbah XXVII:V)

Accordingly, the mode of thought brought to bear upon the theme of history remains exactly the same as before: list-making, with data exhibiting similar taxonomic traits drawn together into lists based on common monothetic traits or definitions. These lists then through the power of repetition make a single enormous point or prove a social law of history. The argument is comprised by a set of established facts, all of which prove the same point, that God favors the pursued over the pursuer. A contrary argument, then, would have to assemble facts to prove the opposite point. Then the second stage would require each party to show that the facts adduced by the other have been improperly classified; the traits of those facts do not conform to the taxon where the item has been situated. So the argument requires classification of facts and then comparison of one set of classified facts with another set.

Reference to established facts commonly invokes facts out of the past. But these facts are treated as timeless, as evidence for propositions that stand beyond the limits of circumstance. The recurrent listing of events subject to a single rule runs as often as possible through the course of all of human history, from creation to the fourth monarchy (Rome), which, everyone knows, is the end of time prior to the age that is coming. Accordingly, the veracity of rabbinic conditional arguments depends over and over again on showing that the condition holds at all times. The proposition of the syllogistic argument at hand derives from clear statements of Scripture, the conditional part: if X, then Y; if not X, then not Y. Lev. 26 (which occupies strikingly slight attention in our composition) states explicitly that if the Israelites keep God's rules, they will prosper, and if not, they will suffer. The viewpoint is commonplace, but its appearance at Leviticus in particular validates the claim that it is topically available to our authors. The two further stages in the encompassing logic of the document do represent a step beyond the simple and commonplace theorem. The first is the construction of the molecular argument, encompassing a broad range of subjects. The second, and the more important of the two, is the insistence of the temporal character of the list. That is why the recurrent reference to sequences of figures, events, or actions, all listed in accord with a monothetic definitive trait, forms so central a component in the argument of the document as a whole. Here is a striking example of that mode of argument. I abbreviate the passage to its main components:

[7A] (Gen. R. 42:2:) Abraham foresaw what the evil kingdoms would do [to Israel].

[B] "[As the sun was going down,] a deep sleep fell on Abraham; [and lo, a dread and great darkness fell upon him]" (Gen. 15:12).

[C] "Dread" (YMH) refers to Babylonia, on account of the statement, "Then Nebuchadnezzer was full of fury (HMH)" (Dan. 3:19).

[D] "Darkness" refers to Media, which brought darkness to Israel through its decrees: "to destroy, to slay, and to wipe out all the Jews" (Est. 7:4).

[E] "Great" refers to Greece.

[J] "Fell on him" (Gen. 15:12).

[K] This refers to Edom, on account of the following verse: "The earth quakes at the noise of their [Edom's] fall" (Jer. 49:21).

[9A] Moses foresaw what the evil kingdoms would do [to Israel].

[B] "The camel, rock badger, and hare" (Deut. 14:7). [Compare: "Nevertheless, among those that chew the cud or part the hoof, you shall not eat these: the camel, because it chews the cud but does not part the hoof, is unclean to you. The rock badger, because it chews the cud but does not part the hoof, is unclean to you. And the hare, because it chews the cud but does not part the hoof, is unclean to you, and the pig, because it parts the hoof and is cloven-footed, but does not chew the cud, is unclean to you" (Lev. 11:4–8).]

[C] The camel (GML) refers to Babylonia [in line with the following verse of Scripture: "O daughter of Babylonia, you who are to be devastated!] Happy will be he who requites (GML) you, with what you have done to us" (Ps. 147:8).

[D] "The rock badger" (Deut. 14:7) – this refers to Media.

[E]   Rabbis and R. Judah b. R. Simon.

[F]   Rabbis say, "Just as the rock badger exhibits traits of
       uncleanness and traits of cleanness, so the kingdom of
       Media produced both a righteous man and a wicked one."

[I]   "The pig" (Deut. 14:7) – this refers to Edom [Rome].

[10A] (Gen. R. 65:1:) R. Phineas and R. Hilqiah in the name of R.
       Simon: "Among all the prophets, only two of them revealed
       [the true evil of Rome], Assaf and Moses.

[B]   Assaf said, 'The pig out of the wood ravages it' (Ps. 80:14).

[C]   Moses said, 'And the pig, [because it parts the hoof and is
       cloven-footed but does not chew the cud]' [Lev. 11:7].

[D]   Why is [Rome] compared to a pig?

[E]   It is to teach you the following: Just as, when a pig crouches
       and produces its hooves, it is as if to say, 'See how I am clean
       [since I have a cloven hoof],' so this evil kingdom acts arro-
       gantly, seizes by violence, and steals, and then gives the
       appearance of establishing a tribunal for justice."

                                        (Leviticus Rabbah XIII:V)

Clearly, we have moved beyond the realm of history, comprised of
one-time, unique participants; now events and parties are turned
into symbols, exemplars of types – the data for social study, not history. In the apocalypticizing of the animals of Lev. 11:4-8 and Deut.
14:7, the camel, rock badger, hare and pig, the pig, standing for
Rome, again emerges as different from the others and more threat-
ening than the rest. Just as the pig pretends to be a clean beast by
showing the cloven hoof, but in fact is an unclean one, so Rome pretends to be just but in fact governs by thuggery. Edom does not
pretend to praise God but only blasphemes. It does not exalt the
righteous but kills them.

The proposition that is demonstrated is clear: after Rome, Israel
will rule. While all the other beasts bring further ones in their wake,
the pig does not: "It does not bring another kingdom after it." It will
restore the crown to the one who will truly deserve it, Israel. Esau will
be judged by Zion (so Obad. 1:21). The argument then is conducted
out of historical facts, and the facts are rendered suitable for the argument by removing facts from their specific contexts and treating
them as exemplary. Now how has the symbolization delivered an
implicit message? It is in the treatment of Rome as distinct, but essentially equivalent to the former kingdoms. This seems to me a
stunning way of saying that the now-Christian empire in no way

requires differentiation from its pagan predecessors. Nothing has changed, except matters have become worse. Beyond Rome, standing in a straight line with the others, lies the true shift in history, the rule of Israel and the cessation of the dominion of the (pagan) nations.

We may now generalize and set forth the character of arguments as represented by Leviticus Rabbah. One paramount mode of argument will invoke events in Israel's history meaning, in this context, Israel's history solely in Scriptural times, down through the return to Zion. The one-time events of the generation of the flood, Sodom and Gomorrah, the patriarchs and the sojourn in Egypt, the exodus, the revelation of the Torah at Sinai, the golden calf, the Davidic monarchy and the building of the Temple, Sennacherib, Hezekiah, and the destruction of northern Israel, Nebuchadnezzar and the destruction of the Temple in 586, the life of Israel in Babylonian captivity, Daniel and his associates, Mordecai and Haman – these events occur over and over again. They turn out to serve as paradigms of sin and atonement, steadfastness and divine intervention, and equivalent lessons. We find, in fact, a fairly standard repertoire of Scriptural heroes or villains, on the one side, and conventional lists of Israel's enemies and their actions and downfall, on the other. The boastful, for instance, include the generation of the flood, Sodom and Gomorrah, Pharaoh, Sisera, Sennacherib, Nebuchadnezzar, the wicked empire (Rome) – contrasted to Israel, "despised and humble in this world." The four kingdoms recur again and again, always ending, of course, with Rome, with the repeated message that after Rome will come Israel. But Israel has to make this happen through its faith and submission to God's will. Lists of enemies ring the changes on Cain, the Sodomites, Pharaoh, Sennacherib, Nebuchadnezzar, Haman.

Accordingly, the mode of thought brought to bear upon the theme of history remains exactly the same as in the Mishnah: list-making, with data exhibiting similar taxonomic traits drawn together into lists based on common monothetic traits or definitions. These lists then through the power of repetition make a single enormous point or prove a social law of history. The catalogues of exemplary heroes and historical events serve a further purpose. They provide a model of how contemporary events are to be absorbed into the biblical paradigm. Since biblical events exemplify recurrent happenings, sin and redemption, forgiveness and atonement, they lose their one-time character. At the same time and in the same way, current events find a place within the ancient, but eternally present, paradigmatic scheme. So no new historical events, other than exemplary episodes in lives of heroes, demand narration because, through what is said about the past, what was happening during the times of the framers of Leviticus Rabbah would also come under consideration. This mode of dealing with biblical history and contemporary events produces two reciprocal effects. The first is the mythicization of biblical stories, their removal from the framework of ongoing, unique patterns of history and sequences of events and their transformation into accounts of things that happen all the time. The second is that contemporary events too lose all of their specificity and enter the paradigmatic framework of established mythic existence. So (1) the Scripture's myth happens every day, and (2) every day produces re-enactment of the Scripture's myth.

The sages at hand pursued a philosophical argument through historical facts. They therefore read the text as if it spoke about something else beyond the specifics at hand, and they read the world as if it lived out the text. At the center of the pretense, that is, the as-if mentality of Leviticus Rabbah and its framers, we find a simple proposition, which contradicted the everyday facts and overturned them: Israel is God's special love. That love is shown in a simple way. Israel's present condition of subordination derives from its own deeds. It follows that God cares, so Israel may look forward to redemption on God's part in response to Israel's own regeneration through repentance. When the exegetes proceeded to open the scroll of Leviticus, they found numerous occasions to state that proposition in concrete terms and specific contexts. The sinner brings on his own sickness, but God heals through that very ailment. The nations of the world govern in heavy succession, but Israel's lack of faith guaranteed their rule and its moment of renewal will end it. Israel's leaders – priests, prophets, kings – fall into an entirely different category from those of the nations, as much as does Israel. In these and other concrete allegations, the same classical message comes forth, but the arguments that validated the message required a revolution in the reading of the past. Specifically, history no longer served as the medium of theology, but only as data for philosophy.

6

ARGUMENTS FROM NATURE
Irenaeus

When Christianity emerged during the second century as a religion distinct from Judaism, other popular movements were also taking shape; taken together the members of those other groups at times greatly outnumbered Christians. Among those movements, the ones called "Gnostic" exerted the strongest influence on the Church, and provided so serious a challenge that Christian theology largely spelled itself out as an alternative to Gnosticism. The debate between Christians and Gnostics enables us clearly to see the articulation of a Christian embrace of the natural world.

The words "Gnostic" and "Gnosticism" derive from the Greek term *gnosis*, which means "knowledge." The knowledge which was in mind in the religious usage of the term was not simply a matter of data or information. Gnostics claimed that they enjoyed insight into the divine realm itself. The origins of Gnosticism have been hotly debated in the history of scholarship. It has been seen to give some examples, as just an elite, intellectual phase within Christianity, or as a typically Hellenistic tendency, or as the transformation of Jewish apocalyptic speculation into a new key. All of those suggestions have merit, but it is not possible to fix upon a single origin of Gnosticism. It is a very widespread phenomenon of the Hellenistic world, and thrived in an environment of syncretism, in which the contributions of many different religions were brought together into new configurations. Gnosticism is one of those syncretistic configurations.

PROLOGUE: PAUL'S DEBATE CONCERNING KNOWLEDGE (GNOSIS)

In his correspondence with Christians in Corinth (1 Cor. and 2 Cor., *c.* 55–56 CE), Paul provides an early indication of the roots of

Oracles had long featured at Delphi, and belief in the possibilities of *communication* with the divine survived skepticism concerning the gods themselves (Apollo, in the case of Delphi). More general communication with the divine realm was offered in the Mysteries: an initiate might join in the release of Persephone from the underworld, or in the rebirth of the dismembered Dionysus. Knowledge of such initiation – which typically involved elaborate and expensive procedures and sacrifices – amounted to direct, unmediated communication with the divine.

Paul is combating just such a purely individualistic understanding of knowledge in the passage from 1 Cor. which we have already considered. Unless love is clearly perceived as the social dimension of God's Spirit within his community, Paul argues that there is no genuine knowledge, which is God's knowing of his own children. For the same reason, Paul will later argue in the most famous chapter of the same letter, "And if I have prophecy and I know all mysteries and all knowledge and if I have all faith so as to move mountains, but I have not love, I am nothing" (1 Cor. 13:2).

THE EMERGENCE OF GNOSTICISM

The quest for knowledge by itself, even knowledge of the divine, is not the same thing as Gnosticism. Rather, Gnosticism represents a further development, a development which successfully competed with Christianity, even as it adopted (and transformed) elements of Christian teaching. The emergence of Gnosticism reflects the appeal of dualism within the period. Dualism refers to any bifurcation of experience into two distinct realms. Gnostics typically made a radical distinction between the present, material world and the ineffable nature of God. This world is subject to decay and the rule of evil forces; only release from it can bring the spiritual awakening and freedom of *gnosis*. Although appeals to the power of *gnosis* such as we have seen disputed by Paul in 1 Cor. were commonly made by the first century, Gnosticism proper with its dualistic emphasis had not yet emerged fully.

Attempts have been made in the past to explain the emergence of Gnosticism on the basis of the apocalyptic literature of Judaism. Apocalypses such as the books of Daniel and *4 Ezra* represent a clear separation between those who are to be saved in a final judgment and those who are to be punished. Similarly, one of the documents found at Qumran, *The War of the Sons of Light and the Sons of Darkness*, provides a clear example of dualism.[2] The whole of Gnosticism can not be explained simply as an inheritance of apocalyptic thought, but its ethical dualism, the hard distinction between the saved and the doomed, does emerge just after the period of the most intense production of apocalypses.

Works such as *4 Ezra* and *2 Baruch* are examples of apocalyptic dualism, and they are joined on the Christian side by the Revelation of John. All were produced after the destruction of the Temple in Jerusalem, which was an incentive to explain how recent history could possibly fit within the overall plan of God. To this list, we should also add *The Testaments of the Twelve Patriarchs*. The work is a composite Judaic and Christian document, reflecting an interest in adding new dimensions of meaning to previously existing text. That is also a characteristic of Gnosticism, which emerged fully during the second century. It is something of an irony that the Roman campaigns in Judaea occasioned a literature which itself helped to push Graeco–Roman religion in a dualistic direction.

A good example of a Gnostic text from the second century is *The Gospel of Truth*, which begins:

> The gospel of truth is a joy for those who have received from the Father of truth the gift of knowing him, through the power of the Word that came forth from the fullness – the one who is in the thought and the mind of the Father, that is, the one who is addressed as the Savior, that being the name of the work he is to perform for the redemption of those who were ignorant of the Father, while the name of the gospel is the proclamation of hope, being discovery for those who search for him.[3]

What is useful about that initial statement is that it is a very simplified summary of major precepts and assumptions of Gnosticism.

"Knowledge" here comes only as a gift of the Father, and is mediated by the "Word," a designation for Jesus taken from the first chapter of John's Gospel. But that Word comes forth from "the fullness," emanations outward from the Father. The complexity of the divine world around the Father is often emphasized in Gnostic texts, and developed to a bewildering degree of detail. The fascination with schemes representing the generation of the world is probably an inheritance from Greek and Roman mythology. The mastery of that detail is held to mean that one has successfully become one who knows, a Gnostic.

A firm distinction is made in *The Gospel of Truth* between those who are spiritual, capable of receiving illumination, and those who are material, ignorant of what is being offered (see *The Gospel of Truth* 28–31). Failure to attain *gnosis*, then, is a mark of one's incapacity to be rescued from the conditions of this world. The assumption throughout is that the material world is a pit of ignorance and decay, from which the Gnostic must be extricated. That explains what is otherwise a puzzling feature of Gnosticism: the wide variance between ascetical self-denial and the encouragement of libertine behavior. In both cases, freedom from what is material was being claimed and put into practice.

Charges against Gnostics of libertinism should not be pressed literally. The same sort of accusations – of such crimes as incest, cannibalism, and debauchery – were brought against Christians during the same period.[4] Both Gnostics and Christians fell under suspicion of beings practitioners of non-traditional religions (superstitions), which would not support the interests of the Empire. Also in both cases, the emphasis upon esoteric doctrine opened the way for the charge that secrecy was intended to conceal something shameful.

Christianity and Gnosticism also challenged the sensibilities of the Graeco-Roman religious philosophies which we have mentioned. During the second century, both of them had discovered the idiom of philosophy itself in order to develop and convey their claims. Particularly, each crafted a distinctive view of the divine "Word" (*Logos*) which conveys the truth of God to humanity. For most Christians, that *Logos* was Jesus Christ, understood as the human teacher who at last fully incarnated what philosophers and prophets had been searching for and had partially seen.

We have already seen, in Chapter 2, how Justin defended his point of view by means of his appropriation of typology in a Pauline vein. In his opposition to the Gnostics, Justin also embraced a millenarian hope of Christianity, in the thousand-year reign of the saints with Christ. That millennium is described in some detail in Rev. 20:1–15:

> And I saw an angel coming down from heaven, having the key of the Abyss and a great chain in his hand. And he grasped the dragon, the ancient serpent, who is the Devil and Satan, and bound him for a thousand years and cast him into the Abyss and locked and sealed it over him, so he could not continue to deceive the nations until the thousand years are finished. After this he must be released for a little time.

And I saw thrones, and judgment was given to those who sat on them, the souls of those who were beheaded for the testimony of Jesus and the word of God, and they who did not worship the beast or his image and did not accept the mark on the forehead and upon the hand. They lived and reigned with Christ a thousand years. The rest of the dead did not live until the thousand years were finished.

This is the first resurrection. Blessed and holy is he who has a share in the first resurrection. Over them the second death has no power, but they will be priests of God and of Christ, and will reign for him for the thousand years. And when the thousand years are finished, Satan will be released from his prison. And he will come forth to deceive the nations on the four corners of the earth – Gog and Magog, whose number is as the sand of the sea – to gather them to war. And they went up over the breadth of the earth and circled the camp of the saints, the beloved city, and fire came down from heaven and consumed them. And the Devil who deceived them was cast into the lake of fire and of sulphur, where the beast and the false prophet are also, and they will be tortured day and night for ever and ever.

And I saw a great white throne and the one who sat upon it, from whose face earth and heaven fled, and there was no place for them. And I saw the dead, the great and the small, standing before the throne. Books were opened, and another book was opened – the book of life; the dead were judged by the things written in the books, according to their deeds. And the sea gave up the dead in it, and death and Hades gave up the dead in them, and they were judged, each according to their deeds. And death and Hades were cast into the lake of fire. This is the second death, the lake of fire. And if anyone was not found written in the book of life, he was cast into the lake of fire.

(Rev. 20:1–15)

Its detailed picture of the end of time and beyond the end of time is precisely what makes the Revelation of John an "apocalypse," a visionary uncovering of the mysterious plan of God. By the time the book was written, around 100 CE, apocalyptic had become a common expression of Christian eschatology.

Jesus' own eschatology was not of an apocalyptic type. His preaching of God's kingdom, although it emphatically included a future dimension, did not involve a precise calendar of the final events of history and of the way God would judge the world. Christianity was like Judaism in the period after 70 CE, when the Temple was destroyed by fire during the Roman siege of Jerusalem, in envisioning the judgment which was to come in increasingly explicit and detailed apocalypses.

Jesus' preaching of the kingdom of God involved a nuanced conception, but his emphasis upon the kingdom as bringing a definitive transformation is evident. The coming of the kingdom, for which his disciples were to pray, meant the "end" of things as they are; their prayer was "eschatological" in that proper sense.

But Jesus' conception was not apocalyptic. An apocalypse, in the manner of the book of Daniel and the Revelation of John in the Bible, exhibits certain characteristic traits. An eschatology, a teaching of the end of things, is typically present, but it is far more detailed in an apocalypse than in the teaching of Jesus. In symbolic language events up to and including the end are described, so that the claim is made that understanding the apocalypse means knowing how and when the definitive judgment of God will be completed. The privilege of the "apocalypse" (which means "revelation" in Greek, *apokalupsis*) is given in the form of a vision. The seer of that vision, who is usually identified as some famous person from the past, is then provided with an interpretation of the meaning of the vision by angelic mediation. The reader or hearer of an apocalypse, then, is put in a position to understand the events of the past and the present on the basis of the future. The vision and the interpretation are provided from heaven, and their truth is attested by a famous figure from the past. And because that figure is from the past, events can be described with accuracy from the time of Daniel in Babylonia (say) until the desecration of the Temple in 167 BCE. That supported the promise that what followed in the vision attributed to Daniel would also prove to be accurate.

Apocalyptic expectation, in the nature of the case, requires to be updated. The victory of the Maccabees during the period in which the book of Daniel was written did not bring with it the definitive victory of Israel, "the saints of the Most High" described in Chapter 7 of Daniel. The Maccabean regime proved to be transient, and the restored Temple, much extended by Herod the Great, was destroyed again in the year 70 CE. Such was the strength of apocalyptic expectation, however, that it remained undefeated by that catastrophe.

Two works in particular demonstrate that apocalyptic expectation continued in both Judaism and Christianity after the disaster of 70

CE. The work called *4 Ezra* (2 Esd. in the Apocrypha) was first produced *c.* 100 CE. Under the authority of Ezra, the scribe of the Torah who brought the Scriptures back from Babylon to Jerusalem, an account of the universal judgment of humanity, on the basis of their relationship towards the Torah, is graphically depicted. Messianic expectation features in the apocalypse, but the emphasis falls unmistakably upon the accountability of all people before God in his final judgment. Near the same time, the Revelation of John was produced. Its focus is more upon the relationship between those who are to be saved of Israel and those who are to be saved of the nations (the gentiles). Rev. 7 envisions just 144,000 people of Israel (from all time, 12,000 from each of the 12 tribes) as "sealed" by an angelic symbol to show that they belong to God (7:1–8). That number is juxtaposed to a numberless throng "from every nation and all tribes, peoples, and languages, standing in front of the throne and before the Lamb" (Rev. 7:9). Here, the perfected number of Israel (twelve times 12,000) is incorporated within the limitless reach of the kingdom.

Both *4 Ezra* and the Revelation of John demonstrate that apocalyptic eschatology thrived within Judaism and Christianity. Both of them also demonstrate that the issue of the Messiah was ancillary to the focus upon ultimate judgment: each envisages only a temporary messianic era, followed by God's further intervention. In *4 Ezra* (7:28), the messianic era is to last 400 years, while it endures 1,000 years in the Revelation (20:4–6). The latter figure is what gives rise to the concern with the Millennium in the apocalyptic vein of Christianity, which continues to this day. But in both cases, that of *4 Ezra* and that of the Revelation, what is striking is that the expectation of the Messiah is not the definitive hope that is envisaged. He is only a part (however important, in the case of Christianity) of the unfolding events.

At precisely the moment that Judaism under the guidance of the Rabbinic ethos moved into the idiom of an ahistorical teleology, Christianity embraced apocalyptic speculation, even at a popular level. The Revelation of John (*c.* 100 CE) and *The Shepherd of Hermas* (*c.* 150 CE) attest the extent to which final judgment became a keen expectation within the early Church. Among the theologians who supported millenarian hope during the second century, Justin and Irenaeus are to be numbered. The challenge which Christianity increasingly faced was to correlate its deep passion for apocalypticism with its even more profound commitment to the Incarnation. If this world is to be swept away in the coming judgment by the Son of

Man, what about those parts of the world which have in fact been incorporated into Christ? In other words: how can the continuing presence of God in the world be reconciled with the radical disruption of that world which is characteristic of apocalyptic expectation?

Millenarianism developed during the second century, particularly in Asia Minor, in response to that question. The visions of the Revelation of John are expressly designated as mediated on the basis of the Spirit (see Rev. 1:10), so that by themselves they do not explain how the flesh in itself is to fair when the envisioned millennium finally arrives. Millenarianism in its various forms insists that the flesh we actually possess is to be transposed into the reign of Christ at the first resurrection.

Justin and his follower Tatian represent this sort of millenarian perfectionism during the second century. Indeed, Tatian, an influential scholar of the early Church, returned to his native Syria and taught the necessity of an asceticism more extreme than was common during the period, even forbidding marriage and any use of wine. Also during the second century, Montanus in Asia Minor claimed that the Spirit of God had entered him to begin a new era of prophecy. That sense of the perfection of a new age seems also to be a reflection of millenarian fervor.

Although Asia Minor and Syria were the especial foci of millenarian expectations, they were readily exported elsewhere. In North Africa, a zealous attitude toward martyrdom is characteristic of the Christianity which flourished there, and may explain why, around 207 CE, even Tertullian became a Montanist, attracted by the asceticism which comported with the conviction that each believer was a vessel of the holy Spirit.

But the extreme emphasis upon the Spirit in the millenarianism of the second century is only one reason for an increasing focus on the question of the flesh. Another is the reaction against Gnosticism. In his response to the claims of Gnosticism, Clement of Alexandria, who was active in the catechetical school in that great city during the latter part of the second century, stands out as a leader among Christians. Alexandria was a center for Gnosticism as well as Christianity, and the two groups contended over a similar constituency. Clement's strategy was to insist that the gospel offered its own *gnosis* in the form of Jesus Christ himself, whom Clement portrayed as *The Paedagogue* (the title of a book he devoted to the theme). That term in Greek had a particular meaning. It did not refer to a school master, but to someone who leads children to school. So

Clement's choice of words conceives of Jesus as a companion on the way to learning. He frames our habits according to divine Wisdom, brings us to the point where we can decide to act according to his word (for he is the *Logos*), and even offers us the prospect of control over our passions.

The role of Christ as the Paedagogue is a daring conception. Clement deliberately avoids the more exalted terminology of divine emanation which had been developed by that time within Gnostic circles. Instead, Clement stresses the offer of mediation to everyone and everything involved in Christ. By choosing an example from a relatively low social status, Clement also hit upon a resonance with the social experience of his own constituency. But that choice had another – and more profound – implication. The Paedagogue who leads the children to school is less exalted than the teacher in the academy, but he also knows those children in ways which the teacher does not. Clement understands Jesus to be involved in the formation of passions, as well as of reason.

Reason is certainly at the center of Clement's view of education. It is the point from which one might decide to learn from the *Logos*. But that decision takes place in a particular social and individual context. Socially, there are habits of behavior and speech which the Paedagogue instills; they are the habits which make the personal decision to learn possible and even likely. Individually, the power of the *Logos* is such that even human passions may fall within its influence. Clement is quite clear that passions are more recalcitrant than reason, and that inadvertent disobedience is inevitable, but he is also insistent in the claim that emotions as well as intellect are reformed in the light of the *Logos*.

Clement's developmental model expresses the anthropology of early Christianity in a way that distinguishes it from Gnosticism. He aggressively reclaims the realm of human passion as part of the potential and actual rule of Christ. Where Gnosticism focuses on the issue of intellectual illumination alone, to the exclusion of the realm of moral and emotional engagement, Christianity during the second century came to insist upon a more integrative understanding of salvation.

Far to the west of Alexandria, in Lyons (in modern France), a contemporary of Clement found a language to describe this integration. Irenaeus, bishop of Lyons, countered Gnostic understandings of the gospel with what was called by his time a "catholic" faith. Faith as catholic is "through the whole" (*kath holou*)[5] of the Church. It is faith such as you would find it in Alexandria, Lyons, Rome, Ephesus, Corinth, Antioch, or wherever. That construction of Christianity is designed to avoid any particular requirement (such as one of the schemes of Gnosticism) being placed upon Christians as such.

Irenaeus' attempt to join in establishing a generic or catholic Christianity called attention to four aspects of faith which have remained constant in classic definitions of Christianity. First, faith was to be expressed by means of the Scriptures as received from Israel; there was no question of eliminating the Hebrew Bible. Second, faith was grounded in the preaching of the apostles, as instanced in their own writings and the creeds. Third, communities were to practice their faith by means of the sacraments which were universally recognized at that time, baptism and eucharist. Fourth, the loyalty of the Church to these principles was to be assured by the authority of bishops and priests, understood as successors of the apostles. Taken together, these were the constituents of "the great and glorious body of Christ." They made the Church a divine institution: "Where the Spirit of God is, there is the Church and all grace, and the Spirit is truth."[6]

Although Irenaeus' conception was designed to be inclusive, it also was at odds with emerging Gnosticism. The issue was not only the authority of the Hebrew Bible (which was typically contested by Gnostics). Gnostics also cherished writings which were not apostolic, sacraments of initiation which were not universal, leaders who were set up privately. The sort of tensions involved might be compared to the relations between adherents of one of the "New Age" movements and Presbyterianism. Although formal exclusion is not in question, neither is one group truly comfortable with the other.

Irenaeus' concern to establish this fourfold definition of the Church is consonant with one of his most vivid observations. Just as there are four quarters of the heavens, four principal winds which circle the world and four cherubim before the throne of God, he says, so there are four Gospels. Indeed, the number four corresponds to the four universal (or catholic) covenants between God and humanity: those of Noah, Abraham, Moses, and Christ.[7] The Gospels belong to the order of the very basics of life, and – what is equally important to appreciate – the basics of life belong to the Gospels. The power of God is not to be abstracted from the terms and conditions of the world in which we live. In insisting upon that, teachers such as Clement and Irenaeus opposed the popular dualism which was a principal appeal of the Gnostics. Instead, catholic Christians insisted upon the Incarnation as the key to the revelation of God's truth to humanity.

The Incarnational emphasis of catholic Christianity is accurately conveyed by its creed, which is still in use under the title, the Apostles' Creed:

> I believe in God the Father almighty,
>   maker of heaven and earth,
> and in Jesus Christ, his only son, our Lord,
>   who was conceived by the holy spirit,
>   born of the virgin Mary,
>   suffered under Pontius Pilate,
>   was crucified, dead, and buried.
>   He descended into hell;
>   the third day he rose from the dead,
>   and ascended into heaven,
>   and sits at the right hand of God the Father almighty.
>   From there he will come to judge
>   the living and the dead.
> I believe in the holy spirit,
>   the holy catholic Church,
>   the communion of saints,
>   the forgiveness of sins,
>   the resurrection of the body,
>   and the life everlasting. Amen.

The division of the creed into three sections, corresponding to Father, Son, and Spirit, is evident. That marks the commitment of catholic Christianity to the Trinity as a means of conceiving God. Its commitment necessitated a philosophical explanation, which Origen ultimately provided (see Chapter 4). Indeed, the Trinity correlates with the kind of Incarnational faith which is expressed in the creed.

The Incarnation refers principally to Jesus as the embodiment of God, from the time of the prologue of John's Gospel (1:1–18). In the creed, however, that view of the Incarnation is developed further. The longest, middle section shows that the ancient practice of Christian catechesis is at the heart of the creed, and that section is a fine summary of the Gospels (compare Peter's speech in Acts 10:34–43). Its level of detail articulates a rigorous alternative to the tendency of Gnosticism toward abstraction. But the statement about Jesus does not stand on its own. His status as son is rooted in the Father's creation of the heavens *and the earth*. The creed begins with an embrace of the God of Israel as creator and with an equally emphatic (if indirect) rejection of dualism.

The last section of the creed, devoted to the Holy Spirit, also recollects the catechesis of Christians which climaxed with baptism and reception of the spirit. That basic understanding is rooted in the catechesis of Peter (again, see Acts 10:34–43, and the sequel in vv. 44–8). But here the common reception of the Spirit is used to assert the communal nature of life in the Spirit. To be baptized is to share the Spirit with the Catholic Church: that is where communion with God and forgiveness are to be found.

Finally, the creed closes on a deeply personal and existential note. "The resurrection of the body" refers, not to Jesus' resurrection (which has already been mentioned), but to the ultimate destiny of all who believe in him. The creed does not spell out its understanding of how God raised Jesus and is to raise us from the dead, but it is unequivocal that we are all to be raised as ourselves, as embodied personalities. There is no trace here of joining an undifferentiated divine entity, or of some part of us (a soul, an essence) surviving in a disembodied way.

In its assertion of the continuity of the body before and after the resurrection, non-Gnostic Christianity came increasingly to stress the complete (that is, material) identity between what had died and what was raised from the dead. Whether the issue was what God raised in the case of Jesus, or what he would raise in the case of believers, material conceptions came to predominate. Resurrection was not merely of the body, the identity which figures in the medium of flesh, but of the flesh itself. The Latin version of the creed actually refers to the resurrection of the flesh at its close.[8] Catholic Christianity emerged as Orthodox at the moment it became credal, and regularized faith in terms of certain opinions (*doxai*) which were held to be right (*ortho-*). That emergence came in the context of opposition to Gnostic versions of Christianity, and the result was the greater attachment to literal, material theologies of the resurrection from the second century onward.

Christianity had attached itself to a profound validation of flesh as a possible vehicle of the divine. From its Incarnational beginnings, the Church had affirmed that God had entered the realm of humanity in the case of Jesus Christ. The corresponding result for those who followed Jesus was, logically, that they could become "participants of the divine nature." That phrase is not a late development within Christianity, but a direct citation from the New Testament (2 Pet. 1:4). But what was not specified by the Incarnational theology of the New Testament was that flesh was to be the method of participation.

From the second century, that became the common understanding (and for that reason the direction of Origen's theology appears all the more starling in the contrast involved).

That understanding involved an implication of the healing qualities of the eucharist, which was taken up and developed by Irenaeus. Irenaeus' appreciation of the eucharist is essentially of the Johannine type, based upon the miraculous provision of bread in chapter 6 (see *Against Heresies* 2.22.3; 3.9.5): here is a blessing for the last times which compares with the miraculous sustenance of Israel. But where eating the bread of life in John results in having eternal life in oneself, for Irenaeus the result is a transformation of one's own flesh.

Irenaeus' insistence upon this notion is inexorable. He is keen to point out that Jesus took bread which had been produced from the earth in order to give thanks in John 6:11 (*Against Heresies* 3.9.5); the same God who creates also redeems, and what he redeems is the flesh of which the bread is a symbol. When Irenaeus speaks of the eucharist itself, he returns to the same theme. Jesus says "This is my body" of bread which had been created in the ordinary way, and its offering is "the new oblation of the new covenant" (*Against Heresies* 4.17.5). The theological significance of this sacrifice is explicated powerfully and simply:

> For as the bread, which is produced from the earth, when it receives the invocation from God, is no longer common bread, but the eucharist, consisting of two realities, earthly and heavenly, so also our bodies, when they receive the eucharist, are no longer corruptible, having the hope of resurrection to eternity.
>
> (*Against Heresies* 4.18.5)

Explicitly and deliberately, Irenaeus makes resurrection into a transformation of human flesh, and eucharist announces "consistently the fellowship and union of the flesh and spirit."

In his treatise *Against Heresies*, Irenaeus pressed the case for the unity implicit in the fulfillment of ancient prophecies in Christ: typology in Irenaeus' treatment became a general theory of the relationship between the Scriptures of Israel and Jesus. It is no coincidence that the second century saw the rise and triumph of the use of the phrase "New Testament" to refer to the canon of the Gospels, the letters and Paul, and the other writings generally received within the Church. That phrase implies another, "Old Testament," which embodies the theory that the Scriptures of Israel are to be understood as types which are fulfilled in Christ. Irenaeus contributed to that early Christian vocabulary of the Scriptures, and even more influentially to the early Christian theory of the Scriptures.

Although Irenaeus made great play of his skepticism of Gnostic speculations, he in fact contributed one of the most daring ideas which Orthodox Christianity accepted, and he did so within his general theory of the Scriptures. Just as he argued for the unity of the Old and the New Testament on the basis of the typology of Hebrews, so Irenaeus developed the relationship between Adam and Christ on the basis of what he read in St. Paul (especially in Rom. 5). The description offered by Henry Chadwick can scarcely be improved upon:

> The divine plan for the new covenant was a "recapitulation" of the original creation. In Christ the divine Word assumed a humanity such as Adam possessed before he fell. Adam was made in the image and likeness of God. By sin the likeness became lost, though the image remained untouched. By faith in Christ mankind may recover the lost likeness. Because Irenaeus regarded salvation as a restoration of the condition prevailing in paradise before the Fall, it was easy for him to accept Justin's terrestrial hopes for the millennium. Because he believed that in the Fall only the moral likeness to God was lost, not the basic image, he was able to regard the Fall in a way very different from the deep pessimism of the Gnostics.[9]

For all his stress upon the authority of apostolic tradition, Irenaeus here shows himself to be one of the great, synthetic philosophers of early Christianity. In a single theory he elevated the flesh to the realm of what may be saved, set out a general approach to the relationship between the Testaments of the Scriptures, and articulated a symmetrical theology of primordial sin and eschatological hope. "God became man that man might become divine" (*Against Heresies* 3.10.2; 3.19.1; 4.33.4, 11). Although there were more creative thinkers in the history of Classical Christianity (such as Origen), and more accomplished theologians (such as Augustine), none was more influential than Irenaeus in his theory of recapitulation. It was a masterful advance along lines already laid down earlier,[10] and Christianity ever since (consciously and not) has been exploring its implications.

The explanation of Irenaeus' lack of historical curiosity is pursued by Lloyd Patterson:

> Irenaeus' lack of interest in *historia* is doubtless due largely to his position on the edge of the world of Hellenistic intellectual ideas in

general. But more than this is to be discerned in his silence. Unwitting though it may have been on his part, he was involved in preparing the way for a renewal of the debate with contemporary philosophy in which accounts of human happenings as such were not likely to play any significant part.[11]

The position of Irenaeus comported with his own background. Unlike Justin before him and Augustine after him, but like Origen in the third century, he was not a convert to Christianity, but a product of Christian culture.

A native of Smyrna in Asia Minor (present-day Turkey), he knew Bishop Polycarp, a great martyr and hero of the faith. Irenaeus' move to Lyons involved him in an embassy to Pope Eleutherus to seek tolerance of the Montanists in Asia Minor. Irenaeus was no Montanist: Montanus, after all, claimed personally to fulfill Jesus' promise of the coming of a *Paraclete* (a "Comforter") in the Gospel according to John (see John 14:16–17, 26; 15:26; 16:7).[12] But Irenaeus' was nurtured in a milieu which anticipated the immediate fulfillment of biblical promises in Christ, and his theory of recapitulation is no historical survey, but an answer to the single question: how is it that faith in Jesus Christ will ultimately transform humanity?

Because recapitulation, like typology, is a theory of salvation, rather than a historical argument, Irenaeus is able to make statements about Jesus without recourse to information about him, even in contradiction of the Gospels. Because Jesus is held to sum up our humanity in his flesh, Irenaeus holds he must have died around the age of fifty, the supposed time of complete human maturity (*Against Heresies* 2.22.1–6). The only reference in the New Testament to Jesus' age comes in the Gospel according to Luke, where he "began to be about thirty" (Luke 3:23) at the start of his ministry. Although that statement is vague, only speculation can turn Jesus' age at his death into fifty. Evidently, the Gnostics were not the only thinkers in the second century who were inventive.

The operative point in the distinction between Irenaeus and the Gnostics he opposed is not that he was historically minded while they embraced philosophy. That once fashionable generalization has virtually no merit. The contrast between them is at once more basic and more interesting. Irenaeus' speculation involved the flesh in its beginning in types, in its recapitulation in the case of Jesus, and in its fulfillment in paradise. Gnostic speculation, by contrast, referred to flesh as an ancillary accident in the overall unfolding of spiritual essence. Because flesh becomes the vehicle of Spirit, in Iranaeus' opinion, Jesus must have been fifty when he died, much as Hebrews can invent elements in Jesus' struggle for obedience. Hebrews' invention of circumstance (the "loud cry" in Gethsemane, see Heb. 5:7–10; see below, p. 155) is less substantial than Irenaeus', but each is motivated by the concern for what must have been the case. And what must have been in the flesh is a projection of what eternally is in heaven.

The procedure of thinking on the basis, not of nature, but of God's essence, and relating that to human nature, is best instanced by Origen. In that sense his procedure moves in a direction different from Irenaeus'. Origen radically challenged the increasing emphasis upon the flesh which was characteristic of Orthodox Christianity in its resistance to Gnosticism. He rather insisted upon the transformation of the idiom of existence from earth to heaven as one imagined the body in which resurrection occurred. The line of demarcation between millenial expectations of eschatology (such as Justin's and Irenaeus') and spiritual expectations of eschatology (such as Clement's and Origen's) is quite clear in classical Christianity, and the difference has yet to be resolved. That is to some extent because arguments from nature and dialectical arguments sometimes render contradictory conclusions.

7

ARGUMENTS FROM SOCIAL HISTORY

Paradigmatic thinking in Ruth Rabbah, Pesiqta deRab Kahana, and Genesis Rabbah

How did history figure in the framing of arguments in Rabbinic Judaism and nascent Christianity? All scholarship on the Hebrew Scriptures concurs that ancient Israel set forth its theology through the media of historical narrative and thought. The Hebrew Scriptures set forth Israel's life as history, with a beginning, middle, and end; a purpose and a coherence; a teleological system. All accounts agree that the Scriptures distinguished past from present, present from future and composed a sustained narrative, made up of one-time, irreversible events. In Scripture's historical portrait, Israel's present condition appealed for explanation to Israel's past, perceived as a coherent sequence of weighty events, each unique, all formed into a great chain of meaning. But that is not how for most of the history of Western civilization the Hebrew Scriptures were read by Judaism and Christianity. The idea of history, with its rigid distinction between past and present and its careful sifting of connections from the one to the other, came quite late onto the scene of intellectual life. Both Judaism and Christianity for most of their histories have read the Hebrew Scriptures in an other-than-historical framework. They found in Scripture's words paradigms of an enduring present, by which all things must take their measure; they possessed no conception whatsoever of the pastness of the past.

Rabbinic Judaism formulated out of Scripture not only rules validated by appeal to arguments resting on facts recorded therein, such as Leviticus Rabbah yields. Rabbinic history's time intersects with, and is superimposed upon, nature's time. Cyclical time forms a modification of history's time, appealing for its divisions of the aggregates of time to the analogy, in human life, to nature's time: the natural sequence of events in a human life viewed as counterpart to the natural sequence of events in solar and lunar time.

So much for a theological formulation of matters. What, in this-worldly language, is to be said about the same conception? Paradigmatic thinking constitutes a mode of argument about the meaning of events, about the formation of the social order. Appealing to the pattern, parties to a debate, for instance about the meaning of an event or the interpretation of a social fact, frame their arguments within the limits of the pattern: that event corresponds to this component of the paradigm shared among all parties to debate. Paradigms derive from human invention and human imagination, imposed on nature and on history alike. Nature is absorbed, history recast, through time paradigmatic; that is, time invented, not time discovered; time defined for a purpose determined by humanity (the social order, the faithful, for instance), time not discovered by determined and predetermined, time that is not natural or formed in correspondence to nature, or imposed upon nature at specified intersections; but time that is defined completely in terms of the prior pattern or the determined paradigm or fabricated model itself: time wholly invented for the purposes of the social order that invents and recognizes time.

Let me make these abstractions concrete, since time paradigmatic refers to perfectly familiar ways of thinking about the passage of time, besides the natural and historical ways of thinking. Once we define time paradigmatic as time invented by humanity for humanity's own purposes, time framed by a system set forth to make sense of a social order, for example, the examples multiply. The use of BC and AD forms one obvious paradigm: all time is divided into two parts by reference to the advent of Jesus Christ. Another paradigm is marked by the history of humanity set forth in Scripture: Eden, then after Eden; or Adam versus Israel, Eden versus the Land; Adam's fall versus Israel's loss of the Land. The sages will impose a further, critical variable on the pattern of Eden versus Land of Israel, Adam versus Israel, and that is, Sinai. A pattern then will recognize the divisions of time between before Sinai and afterward.

These general definitions should be made still more concrete in the setting of Rabbinic Judaism. Let me give a single example of time paradigmatic, in contrast to the conceptions of time that govern in the Hebrew Scriptures. The character of paradigmatic time is captured in the following, which encompasses the entirety of Israel's being (its "history" in conventional language) within the conversation that is portrayed between Boaz and Ruth; we abbreviate the passage to highlight only the critical components:

[XL:i.1A] "And at mealtime Boaz said to her, 'Come here and eat some bread, and dip your morsel in the wine.' So she sat beside the reapers, and he passed to her parched grain; and she ate until she was satisfied, and she had some left over":

[B] R. Yohanan interested the phrase "come here" in six ways:

[C] "The first speaks of David.

[D] 'Come here': means, to the throne: 'That you have brought me here' (2 Sam. 7:18).

[E] '. . . and eat some bread': the bread of the throne.

[F] '. . . and dip your morsel in vinegar': this speaks of his sufferings: 'O Lord, do not rebuke me in your anger' (Ps. 6:2).

[G] 'So she sat beside the reapers': for the throne was taken from him for a time."

[I] and he passed to her parched grain': he was restored to the throne: 'Now I know that the Lord saves his anointed' (Ps. 20:7).

[J] '. . . and she ate and was satisfied and left some over': this indicates that he would eat in this world, in the days of the messiah, and in the age to come."

[2A] "The second interpretation refers to Solomon: 'Come here': means, to the throne.

[B] '. . . and eat some bread': this is the bread of the throne: 'And Solomon's provision for one day was thirty measures of fine flour and three score measures of meal' (1 Kgs. 5:2).

[C] "'. . . and dip your morsel in vinegar': this refers to the dirty of the deeds [that he did].

[D] "'. . . So she sat beside the reapers': for the throne was taken from him for a time."

[G] [Reverting to D]: 'and he passed to her parched grain': for he was restored to the throne.

[H] '. . . and she ate and was satisfied and left some over': this indicates that he would eat in this world, in the days of the messiah, and in the age to come."

[3A] "The third interpretation speaks of Hezekiah: 'Come here': means, to the throne.

[B] '. . . and eat some bread': this is the bread of the throne.

[C] '. . . and dip your morsel in vinegar': this refers to

sufferings [Isa. 5:1]: 'And Isaiah said, Let them take a cake of figs' (Isa. 38:21).

[D]   'So she sat beside the reapers': for the throne was taken from him for a time: 'Thus says Hezekiah, This day is a day of trouble and rebuke' (Isa. 37:3).

[E]   '. . . and he passed to her parched grain': for he was restored to the throne: 'So that he was exalted in the sight of all nations from then on' (2 Chr. 32:23).

[F]   '. . . and she ate and was satisfied and left some over': this indicates that he would eat in this world, in the days of the messiah, and in the age to come.

[4A]   "The fourth interpretation refers to Manasseh: 'Come here': means, to the throne.

[B]   '. . . and eat some bread': this is the bread of the throne.

[C]   '. . . and dip your morsel in vinegar': for his dirty deeds were like vinegar, on account of wicked actions.

[D]   'So she sat beside the reapers': for the throne was taken from him for a time: 'And the Lord spoke to Manasseh and to his people, but they did not listen. So the Lord brought them the captains of the host of the king of Assyria, who took Manasseh with hooks' (2 Chr. 33:10–11). . . ."

[K]   [Reverting to D]: 'and he passed to her parched grain': for he was restored to the throne: 'And brought him back to Jerusalem to his kingdom' (2 Chr. 33:13).

[N]   '. . . and she ate and was satisfied and left some over': this indicates that he would eat in this world, in the days of the messiah, and in the age to come."

[5A]   "The fifth interpretation refers to the Messiah: 'Come here': means, to the throne.

[B]   '. . . and eat some bread': this is the bread of the throne.

[C]   '. . . and dip your morsel in vinegar': this refers to suffering: 'But he was wounded because of our transgressions' (Isa. 53:5).

[D]   'So she sat beside the reapers': for the throne is destined to be taken from him for a time: For I will gather all nations against Jerusalem to battle and the city shall be taken' (Zech. 14:2).

[E]   '. . . and he passed to her parched grain': for he will be restored to the throne: 'And he shall smite the land with the rod of his mouth' (Isa. 11:4).

[I]   [reverting to G]: 'so the last redeemer will be revealed to
        them and then hidden from them.'

(Ruth Rabbah Parashah Five)

The paradigm here may be formed of five units: (1) David's monarchy; (2) Solomon's reign; (3) Hezekiah's reign; (4) Manasseh's reign;
(5) the Messiah's reign. So paradigmatic time compresses events to the
dimensions of its model. All things happen on a single plane of time.
Past, present, future are undifferentiated, and that is why a single
action contains within itself an entire account of Israel's social order
under the aspect of eternity.

The foundations of the paradigm, of course, rest on the fact that
David, Solomon, Hezekiah, Manasseh, and therefore also, the
Messiah, all descend from Ruth's and Boaz's union. Then, within the
framework of the paradigm, the event that is described here – "And at
mealtime Boaz said to her, 'Come here and eat some bread, and dip
your morsel in the wine.' So she sat beside the reapers, and he passed
to her parched grain; and she ate until she was satisfied, and she had
some left over" – forms not an event but a pattern. The pattern transcends time; or more accurately, aggregates of time, the passage of
time, the course of events – these are all simply irrelevant to what is
in play in Scripture. Rather we have a tableau, joining persons who
lived at widely separated moments, linking them all as presences at
this simple exchange between Boaz and Ruth, imputing to them all,
whenever they came into existence, the shape and structure of that
simple moment: the presence of the past, for David, Solomon,
Hezekiah, and so on, but the pastness of the present in which David
or Solomon – or the Messiah for that matter – lived or would live (it
hardly matters; verb tenses prove hopelessly irrelevant to paradigmatic thinking).

Taking account of both the simple example of BC and AD and the
complex one involving the Israelite monarchy and the Messiah, we
ask ourselves how time has been framed within the paradigmatic
mode of thought. The negative is now clear. Paradigmatic time has no
relationship whatsoever to nature's time. It is time invented, not discovered; time predetermined in accord with a model or pattern, not
time negotiated in the interplay between time as defined by nature
and time as differentiated by human cognizance and recognition.

Here the points of differentiation scarcely intersect with either
nature's or history's time; time is not sequential, whether in natural or
historical terms; it is not made up of unique events, whether in nature

or in the social order; it is not differentiated by indicators of a commonplace character. Divisions between past, present, and future lie beyond all comprehension. Natural time is simply ignored here; years do not count, months do not register; the passage of time marked by the sun, correlated with, or ignored by, the course of human events, plays no role at all. All flows from that model – in the present instance, the model of time divided into chapters of Davidic dynastic rulers, time before the Messiah but tightly bound to the person of the Messiah; the division of time here then can take the form of before Boaz's gesture of offering food to Ruth and afterward; before David and after the Messiah; and the like. A variety of interpretation of the passage may yield a range of paradigms; but the model of paradigmatic time will remain one and the same. Not much imagination is required for the invention of symbols to correspond to BC and AD as a medium for expressing paradigmatic time.

The case now permits us further to generalize. The paradigm takes its measures quite atemporally, in terms not of historical movements or recurrent cycles but rather as temporal units of experience, those same aggregates of time, such as nature makes available through the movement of the sun and moon and the passing of the seasons, on the one hand, and through the life of the human being, on the other. A model or pattern or paradigm will set forth an account of the life of the social entity (village, kingdom, people, territory) in terms of differentiated events – wars, reigns, for one example, building a given building and destroying it, for another – yet entirely out of phase with sequences of time.

A paradigm imposed upon time does not call upon the day or month or year to accomplish its task. It will simply set aside nature's time altogether, regarding years and months as bearing a significance other than the temporal one (sequence, span of time, aggregates of time) that history, inclusive of cyclical time's history, posits. Time paradigmatic then views humanity's time as formed into aggregates out of all phase with nature's time, measured in aggregates not coherent with those of the solar year and the lunar month. The aggregates of humanity's time are dictated by humanity's life, as much as the aggregates of nature's time are defined by the course of nature. Nature's time serves not to correlate with humanity's patterns (no longer humanity's time), but rather to mark off units of time to be correlated with the paradigm's aggregates.

It remains to reconsider those systematic comparisons between history's time and other modes of keeping time that have already served us well. Since the comparison of historical and cyclical time is now in hand, let us turn directly to ask: how shall we read the paradigmatic, as distinct from the cyclical mode of formulating a human counterpart to nature's time? Here are the point-by-point correspondences:

1 In time paradigmatic, human events do not form givens, any more than natural events form givens, in the measurement of time; while both of those definitions of the eventful correspond in character to the course of nature, paradigmatic events find their definition in the paradigm, within the logic of the system, in accord with the predetermined pattern, and not in response to the givens of the natural world, whether in the heavens or in the life cycle; paradigmatic time also follows a fixed and predictable pattern, but its identification of what is eventful out of what happens in the world at large derives from its own logic and its own perception; nothing is dictated by nature, not nature's time, not history's time, not the linear progress of historical events, not the cyclical progress of historical patterns.

2 The matter is scarcely adumbrated in the case before us – nature's time plays no independent rule in paradigmatic time; cut down to human size by cyclical time in nature's way, nature's time in paradigmatic thinking is simply absorbed into the system and treated as neutral – nature's time is marked, celebrated, sanctified, but removed from the entire range of history, which is wholly taken over and defined by the paradigm.

3 Consequently, nature's time plays no role in paradigmatic time; time is neither cyclical not linear, it is not marked off by unique events, it is simply neutral and inert. Time is inconsequential; the issue is not whether or not time is reversible in direction from past to future, or whether or not time is to be differentiated (for the same reason) into past, present, and future.

Nature's time, with its sense of forward movement (within the natural analogy supplied by the human life, from birth to death) is simply beyond the paradigmatic limits, for the paradigm admits of neither past nor present nor future, differentiated but also linked, nor cycle and recurrence. These conceptions contradict its very character. A paradigm predetermines, selects happenings in accord with a pattern possessed of its own logic and meaning, unresponsive to the illogic of happenings, whether chaotic, whether orderly, from the human perspective. A model is just that: there to dictate, there to organize, there to take over, make selections, recognize connections, draw

of various sorts, consequential or meaningful events would be selected, and by reference to which these selected events would be shown connected ("meaningful") and explicable in terms of that available logic of paradigm that governed both the making of connections and the drawing of conclusions.

THE PARADIGM OF ISRAEL'S PAST, PRESENT, AND FUTURE (= "HISTORY" IN THE COUNTERPART STRUCTURE OF HISTORICAL THINKING): how shall we organize happenings into events? On the largest scale the question concerns the division into periods not of sequences but of mere sets of happenings. Periodization involves explanation, of course, since even in a paradigmatic structure, once matters are set forth as periods, then an element of sequence is admitted into the processes of description and therefore analysis and explanation.

ISRAEL AND THE NATIONS: moving from large aggregates, bordering on abstraction, we turn to the very concrete question of how Israel relates to the rest of the world. This involves explaining not what happened this morning in particular, but what always happens, that is, defining the structure of Israel's life in the politics of this world, explaining the order of things in both the social, political structure of the world and also the sequence of actions that may occur and recur over time (the difference, paradigmatically, hardly matters).

EXPLAINING THE PATTERN OF EVENTS: MAKING CONNECTIONS, DRAWING CONCLUSIONS: paradigmatic thinking, no less than historical, explains matters; but the explanation derives from the character of the pattern, rather than the order of events, which governs historical explanation. Connections then that are drawn between one thing and something else serve to define a paradigm, rather than to convey a temporal explanation based on sequences, first this, then that, therefore this explains why that happened. The paradigm bears a different explanation altogether, one that derives from its principle of selection, and therefore the kinds of explanations paradigmatic thinking sets forth, expressed through its principles of selection in making connections and drawing conclusions, will demand rich instantiation.

THE FUTURE HISTORY OF ISRAEL: just as studying the past is supposed to explain the present and point to the future – surely the rationale for historical thinking and writing, as the account in Chapter 1 of principles of history in the Hebrew Scriptures showed us – so paradigmatic thinking bears the same responsibility. That concerns not so much explaining the present as permitting informed speculation about what will happen in the future. And that speculation will appeal to those principles of order, structure, and explanation that the paradigm sets forth to begin with. So future history in historical thinking and writing projects out of past and present a trajectory over time to come, and future history in paradigmatic thinking forms projects along other lines altogether.

The paradigm does its work on all data, without regard to scale or context or circumstance. What this means is that any paradigmatic case – personality, event, idea – imposes structure and order on all data; and the structure will be the same for the small and the large, the now and the then. By that criterion of paradigmatic structuring of "history," we should be able to tell the story of Israel's past, present, and future, by appeal to any identified model, and what we need not predict is which model will yield which pattern, for the patterns are always the same, whatever the choice of the model. In the following, for a striking example, we are able to define the paradigm of Israel's history out of the lives of the founders of the Israelite tribes. That is not a matter of mere generalities. The tribal progenitors moreover correspond to the kingdoms that will rule over Israel, so there is a correspondence of opposites. In the following, as the single best formulation of paradigmatic thinking in the Rabbinic canon, Israel's history is taken over into the structure of Israel's life of sanctification, and all that happens to Israel forms part of the structure of holiness built around cult, Torah, synagogue, sages, Zion, and the like. I present only a small part:

[2A] "As he looked, he saw a well in the field":

[B]   R. Hama bar Hanina interpreted the verse in six ways [that is, he divides the verse into six clauses and systematically reads each of the clauses in light of the others and in line with an overriding theme:

[C]   "'As he looked, he saw a well in the field': this refers to the well [of water in the wilderness, Num. 21:17].

[D]   '. . . and lo, three flocks of sheep lying beside it': specifically, Moses, Aaron, and Miriam.

[E]   '. . . for out of that well the flocks were watered': from there each one drew water for his standard, tribe, and family."

[F]   'And the stone upon the well's mouth was great:"

[G]   Said R. Hanina, "It was only the size of a little sieve."

[H]   [Reverting to Hama's statement]: "'. . . and put the stone back in its place upon the mouth of the well': for the coming journeys. [Thus the first interpretation applies the passage at hand to the life of Israel in the wilderness.]

[3A] 'As he looked, he saw a well in the field': refers to Zion.

[B] '... and lo, three flocks of sheep lying beside it': refers to the three festivals.

[C] '... for out of that well the flocks were watered': from there they drank of the holy spirit.

[D] '... The stone on the well's mouth was large': this refers to the rejoicing of the house of the water-drawing."

[E] Said R. Hoshaiah, "Why is it called 'the house of the water drawing'? Because from there they drink of the Holy Spirit."

[F] [Resuming Hama b. Hanina's discourse]: "'... and when all the flocks were gathered there': coming from 'the entrance of Hamath to the brook of Egypt' (1 Kgs. 8:66).

[G] '... the shepherds would roll the stone from the mouth of the well and water the sheep': for from there they would drink of the Holy Spirit.

[H] '... and put the stone back in its place upon the mouth of the well': leaving it in place until the coming festival. [Thus the second interpretation reads the verse in light of the Temple celebration of the Festival of Tabernacles.]

[5A] 'As he looked, he saw a well in the field': this refers to Zion.

[B] '... and lo, three flocks of sheep lying beside it': this refers to the first three kingdoms [Babylonia, Media, Greece].

[C] '... for out of that well the flocks were watered': for they enriched the treasures that were laid upon up in the chambers of the Temple.

[D] '... The stone on the well's mouth was large': this refers to the merit attained by the patriarchs.

[E] '... and when all the flocks were gathered there': this refers to the wicked kingdom, which collects troops through levies over all the nations of the world.

[F] '... the shepherds would roll the stone from the mouth of the well and water the sheep': for they enriched the treasures that were laid upon up in the chambers of the Temple.

[G] '... and put the stone back in its place upon the mouth of the well': in the age to come the merit attained by the patriarchs will stand [in defense of Israel]." [So the fourth interpretation interweaves the themes of the Temple cult and the domination of the four monarchies.]

[7A] 'As he looked, he saw a well in the field': this refers to the synagogue.

[B] '. . . and lo, three flocks of sheep lying beside it': this refers to the three who are called to the reading of the Torah on weekdays.

[C] '. . . for out of that well the flocks were watered': for from there they hear the reading of the Torah.

[D] '. . . The stone on the well's mouth was large': this refers to the impulse to do evil.

[E] '. . . and when all the flocks were gathered there': this refers to the congregation.

[F] '. . . the shepherds would roll the stone from the mouth of the well and water the sheep': for from there they hear the reading of the Torah.

[G] '. . . and put the stone back in its place upon the mouth of the well': for once they go forth [from the hearing of the reading of the Torah] the impulse to do evil reverts to its place." [The sixth and last interpretation turns to the twin themes of the reading of the Torah in the synagogue and the evil impulse, temporarily driven off through the hearing of the Torah.]

(Genesis Rabbah LXX:VIII)

So much for the correlation of the structures of the social and cosmic order with the condition of Israel. In the passage just reviewed, paradigms take over the organization of events. Time is no longer sequential and linear. What endures are the structures of cosmos and society: prophets, Zion, sanhedrin, holy seasons, and on and on. Clearly, the one thing that plays no role whatsoever in this tableau and frieze is Israel's linear history; past and future take place in an eternal present.

That formulation, however, cannot complete the picture, since Israel's experience encompasses the nations, on the one side, Rome, on the other. Any claim to classify spells of time has to take account of the worldly political experience of Israel; that, after all, is what sets the agenda of thought to begin with. The periodization of history can be worked out in terms of Rome's rule now, Israel's dominance in the age to come. The comparability of the two is expressed in various ways, for example:

[2A] "Two nations are in your womb, [and two peoples, born of you, shall be divided; the one shall be stronger than the other, and the elder shall serve the younger] (Gen. 25:23).

[B]   There are two proud nations in your womb, this one takes
        pride in his world, and that one takes pride in his world.

[C]   This one takes pride in his monarchy, and that one takes
        pride in his monarchy.

[D]   There are two proud nations in your womb.

[E]   Hadrian represents the nations, Solomon, Israel.

[F]   There are two who are hated by the nations in your womb.
        All the nations hate Esau, and all the nations hate Israel.

[G]   The one whom your creator hates is in your womb: 'And
        Esau I hated'" (Mal. 1:3).

                                        (Genesis Rabbah LXIII:VII)

Thus far, paradigmatic thinking has come to expression in the transformation of actions or traits of the patriarchs into markers of time,
modes of the characterization of what history treats as historical. But
any conception that thinking about social experience by appeal to
patterns or models, rather than sequences in teleological order,
requires attention to data of a narrowly historical character, for example, persons or events paradigmatized, misconstrues the character of
the mode of thinking that is before us. We may indeed make sense of
Israel's social world by appeal to the deeds or traits of the patriarchs
or tribal progenitors. But other statements of the Torah serve equally
well as sources for paradigmatic interpretation: models of how things
are to be organized and made sensible, against which how things
actually are to be measured.

The purpose of paradigmatic thinking, as much as historical
thinking, points toward the future. History is important to explain
the present, also to help peer into the future; and paradigms serve
precisely the same purpose. The choice between the one model and
the other, then, rests upon which appeals to the more authentic
data. In that competition Scripture, treated as paradigm, met no
competition in linear history, and it was paradigmatic, not historical,
thinking that proved compelling for a thousand years or more. The
future history of Israel is written in Scripture, and what happened in
the beginning is what is going to happen at the end of time. That
sense of order and balance prevailed. It comes to expression in a variety of passages, of which a severely truncated selection will have to
suffice:

[2A]   Said R. Abin, "Just as [Israel's history] began with the
        encounter with four kingdoms, so [Israel's history] will con-
        clude with the encounter with the four kingdoms.

[B] 'Chedorlaomer, king of Elam, Tidal, king of Goiim, Amraphel, king of Shinar, and Arioch, king of Ellasar, four kings against five' (Gen. 14:9).

[C] So [Israel's history] will conclude with the encounter with the four kingdoms: the kingdom of Babylonia, the kingdom of Medea, the kingdom of Greece, and the kingdom of Edom."

(Genesis Rabbah XLII:II)

Another pattern serves as well, resting as it does on the foundations of the former. It is the familiar one that appeals to the deeds of the founders. The lives of the patriarchs stand for the history of Israel; the deeds of the patriarchs cover the future historical periods in Israel's destiny.

A single formulation of matters suffices to show how the entire history of Israel was foreseen at the outset:

[1A] R. Hiyya taught on Tannaite authority, "At the beginning of the creation of the world the Holy One, blessed be He, foresaw that the Temple would be built, destroyed, and rebuilt.

[B] "'*In the beginning God created the heaven and the earth*' (Gen. 1:1) [refers to the Temple] when it was built, in line with the following verse: '*That I may plant the heavens and lay the foundations of the earth and say to Zion, You are my people*' (Isa. 51:16).

[C] "'*And the earth was unformed*' – lo, this refers to the destruction, in line with this verse: '*I saw the earth, and lo, it was unformed*' (Jer. 4:23).

[D] "'*And God said, Let there be light*' – lo, it was built and well constructed in the age to come."

(Pesiqta deRab Kahana XXI:V)

A single specific example of the foregoing proposition suffices. It is drawn from that same mode of paradigmatic thinking that imposes the model of the beginning upon the end. In the present case the yield is consequential: we know what God is going to do to Rome. What God did to the Egyptians foreshadows what God will do to the Romans at the end of time. What we have here is the opposite of cyclical history; here history conforms to a pattern, end-time recapitulated creation's events and complementing them; here we see a good example of how paradigmatic thinking addresses the possibility of cyclicality and insists instead upon closure:

[A] R. Levi in the name of R. Hama bar Hanina: "He who

exacted vengeance from the former [oppressor] will exact vengeance from the latter.

[B]   Just as, in Egypt, it was with blood, so with Edom it will be the same: '*I will show wonders in the heavens and in the earth, blood, and fire, and pillars of smoke*' (Job 3:3).

[C]   Just as, in Egypt, it was with frogs, so with Edom it will be the same: '*The sound of an uproar from the city, an uproar because of the palace, an uproar of the Lord who renders recompense to his enemies*' (Isa. 66:6).

[D]   Just as, in Egypt, it was with lice, so with Edom it will be the same: '*The streams of Bosrah will be turned into pitch, and the dust thereof into brimstone, and the land thereof shall become burning pitch*' (Isa. 34:9). '*Smite the dust of the earth that it may become lice*' (Exod. 8:12).

[E]   Just as, in Egypt, it was with swarms of wild beasts, so with Edom it will be the same: '*The pelican and the bittern shall possess it*' (Isa. 34:11).

[F]   Just as, in Egypt, it was with pestilence, so with Edom it will be the same: '*I will plead against Gog with pestilence and with blood*' (Ezek. 38:22).

[G]   Just as, in Egypt, it was with boils, so with Edom it will be the same: '*This shall be the plague wherewith the Lord will smite all the peoples that have warred against Jerusalem: their flesh shall consume away while they stand upon their feet*' (Zech. 14:12).

[H]   Just as, in Egypt, it was with great stones, so with Edom it will be the same: '*I will cause to rain upon Gog . . . an overflowing shower and great hailstones*' (Ezek. 38:22).

[I]   Just as, in Egypt, it was with locusts, so with Edom it will be the same: '*And you, son of man, thus says the Lord God: Speak to birds of every sort...the flesh of the mighty shall you eat...blood shall you drink...you shall eat fat until you are full and drink blood until you are drunk*' (Ezek. 39:17–19).

[J]   Just as, in Egypt, it was with darkness, so with Edom it will be the same: '*He shall stretch over Edom the line of chaos and the plummet of emptiness*' (Isa. 34:11).

[K]   Just as, in Egypt, he took out their greatest figure and killed him, so with Edom it will be the same: '*A great slaughter in the land of Edom, among them to come down shall be the wild oxen*'" (Isa. 34:6–7).

(Pesiqta deRab Kahana VII:XI.3)

The exposition of matters through the small sample given here leaves no doubt on precisely how paradigmatic thinking recast Israel's recorded experience ("history") into a set of models that pertained everywhere and all the time. The picture does not change in the final set of documents, which we shall survey only cursorily.

This survey of the way in which paradigmatic thinking comes to expression now permits a more general statement of matters. As a medium of organizing and accounting for experience, history – the linear narrative of singular events intended to explain how things got to their present state and therefore why – does not enjoy the status of a given. Nor does historical thinking concerning the social order self-evidently lay claim on plausibility. It is one possibility among many. For reasons proposed in the opening chapter, historical thinking – sequential narrative of one-time events – presupposes order, linearity, distinction between time past and time present, and teleology, among data that do not self-evidently sustain such presuppositions. Questions of chaos intervene; the very possibility of historical narrative meets a challenge in the diversity of story-lines, the complexity of events, the bias of the principle of selection of what is eventful, of historical interest, among a broad choice of happenings: why this, not that. Narrative history first posits a gap between past and present, but then bridges the gap; why not entertain the possibility that to begin with there is none? These and similar considerations invite a different way of thinking about how things have been and now are, a different tense structure altogether.

A way of thinking about the experience of humanity, whether past or contemporary, that makes other distinctions from the historical ones between past and present and that eschews linear narrative and so takes account of the chaos that ultimately prevails, now competes with historical thinking. Paradigmatic thinking, a different medium for organizing and explaining things that happen, deals with the same data that occupy historical thinking, and that is why when we refer to paradigmatic thinking, the word "history" gains its quotation marks: it is not a datum of thought, merely a choice; contradicting to its core the character of paradigmatic thinking, the category then joins its opposite paradigm, only by forming the oxymoron before us: paradigmatic thinking *about* "history."

The category, "history," as conventionally defined and as further realized in the Authorized History of Scripture, Genesis through to Kings, therefore forms merely one way of addressing the past in order to find sense and meaning therein. Clearly, with its emphasis on linear, irreversible events and the division between past and present, history's (that is, as conceived historically) is not the way taken by Rabbinic Judaism in organizing Israel's experience: selecting what matters and explaining it. We know that that is the fact because none of the indicators of historical writing and thinking come to the surface in the documents under study. The very opposite traits predominate. Rabbinic literature contains no sustained historical or biographical narrative, only anecdotes, makes no distinction between past and present but melds them. But that writing, resting as it does on the Hebrew Scriptures, then presents a paradox. A set of writings of a one-sidedly historical character, the Hebrew Scripture deriving from ancient Israel finds itself expounded in an utterly ahistorical way by its heirs, both Judaic and Christian.

For, it is clear, the records represented as recording events of the past – the written Torah, the Old Testament – form a massive presence in Judaism and Christianity respectively. So history in the conventional sense formed a principal mode of thinking in the documents that educated the framers of the dual Torah of Judaism and the Bible of Christianity. It must follow, both of those religions defined as an important component of God's revelation to humanity documents that, by all accounts, constituted systematic statements of the past: history-books above all else. But, we shall now see, these accounts of the past, received into the entire Torah, oral and written, of Judaism, and into the Bible, Old and New Testaments, of Christianity, received a reading that we define as one of a paradigmatic character. Given the fundamentally historical character of the Hebrew Scriptures transformed into written Torah and Old Testament, respectively, we must identify the basis for the rereading imposed thereon by the heirs.

That is to say, what Scripture ("written Torah," "Old Testament") yields for Rabbinic Judaism is not one-time events, arranged in sequence to dictate meaning, but models or patterns of conduct and consequence. These models are defined by the written Torah or the Old Testament (read in light of the perspective of the Oral Torah or the New Testament). No component of the paradigm we shall consider emerges from other than the selected experience set forth by Scripture. But the paradigms are at the same time pertinent without regard to considerations of scale and formulated without interest in matters of singular context. Forthrightly selective – this matters, that is ignored – the principle of selection is not framed in terms of sequence; order of a different sort is found.

The models or paradigms that are so discerned then pertain not to one time alone – past time – but to all times equally – past, present and future. Hence "time" no longer forms an organizing category of understanding and interpretation. The spells marked out by moon and sun and fixed stars bear meaning, to be sure. But that meaning has no bearing upon the designation of one year as past, another as present. The meaning imputed to the lunar and solar marking of time derives from the cult, on the one side, and the calendar of holy time, on the other: seven solar days, a Sabbath; a lunar cycle, a new month to be celebrated, the first new moon after the vernal equinox, the Passover, and after the autumnal, Tabernacles. Rabbinic Judaism tells time the way nature does and only in that way; events in Rabbinic Judaism deemed worth recording in time take place the way events in nature do. What accounts for the difference, between history's time and paradigmatic time as set forth here, is a conception of time quite different from the definition of historical time that operates in Scripture – the confluence of nature's time and history's way of telling time – two distinct chronographies brought together, the human one then imposed upon the natural one.

In Rabbinic Judaism the natural way of telling time precipitated celebration of nature. True, those same events were associated with moments of Israel's experience as well: the exodus above all. The language of prayer, for example, the Sabbath's classification as a memorial to creation and also a remembrance of the exodus from Egypt, leaves no doubt about the dual character of the annotation of time. But the exodus, memorialized hither and yon through the solar seasons and the Sabbath alike, constituted no more a specific, never-to-be-repeated, one-time historical event, part of a sustained narrative of such events, than any other moment in Israel's time, inclusive of the building and the destruction of the Temple. Quite to the contrary, linking creation and exodus classified both in a single category; the character of that category – historical or paradigmatic – is not difficult to define; the exodus is treated as consubstantial with creation, a paradigm, not a one-time event.

It follows that this Judaism's Israel kept time in two ways, and the one particular to Israel (in the way in which the natural calendar was not particular to Israel) through its formulation as a model instead of a singular event was made to accord with the natural calendar, not vice versa. That is to say, just as the natural calendar recorded time that was the opposite of historical, because it was not linear and singular and teleological but reversible and repetitive, so Israel kept time with reference to events, whether past or present, that also were not singular, linear, or teleological. These were, rather, reconstitutive in the forever of here and now – not a return to a perfect time but a recapitulation of a model forever present. Israel could treat as comparable the creation of the world and the exodus from Egypt (as the liturgy commonly does, for example, in connection with the Sabbath) because Israel's paradigm (not "history") and nature's time corresponded in character, were consubstantial and not mutually contradictory, in the terms introduced in Chapters 1 and 2.

And that consubstantiality explains why paradigm and natural time work so well together. Now, "time" bears a different signification. It is here one not limited to the definition assigned by nature – yet also not imposed upon natural time but treated as congruent and complementary with nature's time. How so? Events – things that happen that are deemed consequential – are eventful, meaningful, by a criterion of selection congruent in character with nature's own. To understand why that is so, we must recall the character of the Torah's paradigms:

(1) Scripture set forth certain patterns which, applied to the chaos of the moment, selected out of a broad range of candidates some things and omitted reference to others.

(2) The selected things then are given their structure and order by appeal to the paradigm, indifference to scale forming the systemic counterpart to the paradigm's indifference to context, time, circumstance.

(3) That explains how some events narrated by Scripture emerged as patterns, imposing their lines of order and structure upon happenings of other times.

And this yields the basis for the claim of consubstantiality: (4) Scripture's paradigms – Eden, the Land – appealed to nature in another form.

The upshot, then, we state with heavy emphasis: *the rhythms of the sun and moon are celebrated in the very forum in which the Land, Israel's Eden, yields its celebration to the Creator.* The rhythmic quality of the paradigm then compares with the rhythmic quality of natural time: not cyclical, but also not linear. Nature's way of telling time and the Torah's way meet in the Temple: its events are nature's, its story a tale of nature too. Past and present flow together and join in future time too because, as in nature, what is past is what is now and what will be. The paradigms, specified in a moment, form counterparts to the significations of nature's time.

These events of Israel's life (we cannot now refer to Israel's "history") – or, rather, the models or patterns that they yielded – served as the criteria for selection, among happenings of any time, past, present, or future, of the things that mattered out of the things that did not matter: a way of keeping track, a mode of marking time. The model or paradigm that set forth the measure of meaning then applied whether to events of vast consequence or to the trivialities of everyday concern alone. Sense was where sense was found by the measure of the paradigm; everything else lost consequence. Connections were then to be made between this and that, and the other thing did not count. Conclusions then were to be drawn between the connection of this and that, and no consequences were to be imputed into the thing that did not count.

That is not an ideal way of discovering or positing order amid chaos; much was left, if not unaccounted for, then not counted to begin with. We cannot take for granted that the range of events chosen for paradigms struck everyone concerned as urgent or even deserving of high priority, and we must also assume that other Israelites, besides those responsible for writing and preserving the books surveyed here, will have identified other paradigms altogether. But – for those who accorded to these books authority and self-evidence – the paradigm encompassing the things that did conform to the pattern and did replicate its structure excluded what it did not explain. So it left the sense that while chaos characterized the realm beyond consciousness, the things of which people took cognizance also made sense – a self-fulfilling system of enormously compelling logic. For the system could explain what it regarded as important, and also dismiss what it regarded as inconsequential or meaningless, therefore defining the data that fitted and dismissing those that did not.

At stake in the paradigm is discerning order and regularity not everywhere – in the setting of these books, "everywhere" defied imagining – but in some few sets of happenings. The scale revised both upward and downward the range of concern: these are not all happenings, but they are the ones that matter – and they matter very much. Realizing or replicating the paradigm, they uniquely constitute events, and, that is why by definition, these are the only events that matter. Paradigmatic thinking about past, present, and future ignores issues of linear order and temporal sequence because it recognizes another logic altogether, besides the one of priority and posteriority and causation formulated in historical terms.

That mode of thinking, as its name states, appeals to the logic of models or patterns that serve without regard to time and circumstance on the one side, or scale on the other. The sense for order unfolds, first of all, through that logic of selection that dictates what matters and what does not. And, out of the things that matter, that same logic defines the connections of things, so forming a system of description, analysis, and explanation that consists in the making of connections between this and that, but not the other thing, and the drawing of conclusions from those ineluctable, self-evident connections. At stake now is the definition of self-evidence: how did our sages know the difference between a paradigmatic event and a mere happening?

When we speak of the presence of the past, we raise not generalities or possibilities but the concrete experience that generations actively mourning the Temple endured. When we speak of the pastness of the present, we describe the consciousness of people who could open Scripture and find themselves right there, in its record – not only Lamentations, but also prophecy and, especially, in the books of the Torah. Here we deal not with the spiritualization of Scripture, but with the acutely contemporary and immediate realization of Scripture: once again, as then; Scripture in the present day, the present day in Scripture. That is why it was possible for sages to formulate out of Scripture a paradigm that imposed structure and order upon the world that they themselves encountered.

Since, then, sages did not see themselves as removed in time and space from the generative events to which they referred the experience of the here and now, they also had no need to make the past contemporary. If the exodus was irreversible, a once-for-all-time event, then, as we see, our sages saw matters in a different way altogether. They neither relived nor transformed one-time historical events, for they found another way to overcome the barrier of chronological separation. Specifically, if history began when the gap between present and past shaped consciousness, then we naturally ask ourselves whether the point at which historical modes of thought concluded and a different mode of thought took over produced an opposite consciousness from the historical one: not cycle but paradigm. For, it seems to me clear, the premise that time and space separated our sages of the Rabbinic writings from the great events of the past simply did not win attention. The opposite premise defined matters: barriers of space and time in no way separated sages from great events, the great events of the past enduring for all time. How then are we to account for this remarkably different way of encounter, experience, and, consequently, explanation? The answer has already been adumbrated.

Sages assembled in the documents of Rabbinic Judaism, from the Mishnah forward, all recognized the destruction of the Second Temple and all took for granted that that event was to be understood by reference to the model of the destruction of the first. A variety of sources reviewed here maintains precisely that position and expresses it in so many words, for example, the colloquy between Aqiba and sages about the comfort to be derived from the ephemeral glory of Rome and the temporary ruin of Jerusalem. It follows that for our sages of blessed memory, the destruction of the Temple in 70 CE did not mark a break with the past, such as it had for their predecessors some 500 years earlier, but rather a recapitulation of the past. Paradigmatic thinking then began in that very event that precipitated thought about history to begin with, the end of the old order. But paradigm replaced history because what had taken place the first time as unique and unprecedented took place the second time in precisely the same pattern and therefore formed of an episode a series. Paradigmatic thinking replaced historical thinking when history, as an account of one-time, irreversible, unique events, arranged in linear sequence and pointing toward a teleological conclusion, lost all plausibility. If the first time around, history – with the past marked off from the present, events arranged in linear sequence, narrative of a sustained character serving as the medium of thought – provided the medium for making sense of matters, then the second time around, history lost all currency.

The real choice facing our sages was not linear history as against paradigmatic thinking, but rather, paradigm as against cycle. For the conclusion to be drawn from the destruction of the Temple once again, now that history, its premises disallowed, yielded no explanation, can have taken the form of a theory of the cyclicality of events. As nature yielded its spring, summer, fall and winter, so the events of humanity or of Israel in particular can have been asked to conform to a cyclical pattern in line, for example, with Qohelet's view that what has been is what will be. But our sages obviously did not take that position at all.

They rejected cyclicality in favor of a different ordering of events altogether. They did not believe the Temple would be rebuilt and destroyed again, rebuilt and destroyed, and so on into endless time. They stated the very opposite: the Temple would be rebuilt but never again destroyed. And that represented a view of the second destruction that rejected cyclicality altogether. Sages instead opted for

ARGUMENTS FROM SOCIAL HISTORY

Paradigmatic thinking in Augustine

Christianity in its primitive phase of development was a movement, or a collection of movements, within Judaism. That was both its perception of itself and the way it was generally seen by outsiders. The claim of the first followers of Jesus was that they were the true Israel, and they took for granted the normative status of the Scriptures of Israel.[1] In Chapter 2, we saw how the Epistle to the Hebrews reads the Scriptures of Israel as the foreshadowed truth of what Jesus, the great high priest, fully reveals. What came before Jesus were types of the truth, while Jesus himself is the substance of truth.

The power of the contribution of the Epistle to the Hebrews resides in its use of the idea and method of types in order to explain how Jesus was related to the Scriptures of Israel. Within the catechesis of primitive Christianity it had already been a matter of consensus that there was such an analogy between Christ and the Scriptures. The frequent reference back to the Scriptures of Israel within the Gospels is eloquent testimony to that. Hebrews, therefore, was not influential because its reading of Christ's significance was totally unique. Rather, its development of typology explained how there could be a constant analogy between Christ and Scripture on the basis of a single way of reading the text and experiencing Jesus.

In that Jesus is the key to understanding the Scripture, Scripture may also be used to illuminate the significance of Jesus. That is the method of Hebrews, and its execution became classic because its method was taken up and elaborated in later centuries. Hebrews' focus was upon Jesus Christ as "yesterday and today the same, and forever" (Heb. 13:8).

A similar indifference to what we would call history was expressed by Paul: "So we from now on regard no one according to the flesh; although we once regarded Christ according to the flesh, we no longer regard him in that way" (2 Cor. 5:16). In his judicious commentary, Victor Paul Furnish paraphrases Paul's concern as "to emphasize that for the Christian no *worldly standards have any proper role in the evaluation of other persons* (v.16*a*), since they certainly play no role in one's evaluation of Christ (v.16*b*)."[2]

Paul's conviction that, somehow, Christ was to be the standard of everything we might know and do was developed in Hebrews by means of its theory and method of typology. The genius of Hebrews was that it could explain and explore the insight which Paul (however brilliantly) could only assert and stress. Types provided the link between Jesus and the Scriptures of Israel, while insisting upon the prior importance of the Son to any ancillary testimony to the will and purposes of God.

The relative sophistication of Hebrews, however, in no way implies that its stance is more historical than Paul's, or than that of primitive Christianity as a whole. In Chapter 5, Jesus is referred to under the figure of Melchizedek in the book of Psalms, and then immediate reference is made to his passion:

> In the days of his flesh, he offered prayers and supplications, with a strong cry and tears, to the one who was able to save him from death, and he was heard for his piety . . .

> (Heb. 5:7)

A connection between this statement and the Synoptic description of Jesus in Gethsemane (Matt. 26:36–46; Mark 14:32–42; Luke 22:39–46) has frequently been observed. But in the Synoptic passages, no "loud cry" is at issue; Hebrews is enhancing the scene, in the interests of its christology of the significance of Jesus' suffering (see Heb. 5:8). The eternal significance of Jesus means that some things must have been so "in the days of his flesh." Just as Hebrews articulates Jesus' eternal status in the mind of primitive Christianity and early Christianity, so it articulates the corollary motif: what is eternally true about Jesus must in some way have been reflected in the course of his physical life.

In many ways, of course, assertions of what must have been the case during Jesus' life will give the appearance of what we call history. The first two chapters of Luke, for example, provide what seem superficially to be circumstantial reports concerning Jesus' birth. But at many points, the Lukan chapters contradict the opening chapters of Matthew. For example, when Jesus' family is fleeing to Egypt in Matt. (2:13–15), they are circumcising the child and bringing him to

Jerusalem to present him at the Temple in Luke (2:21–24). In addition, of course, Luke has the characters speak in psalmic arias, which are still used as part of Christian worship, and which probably originated in that setting. The point about such material is not that it is a simple matter of legend. Rather, circumstantial material speaks of the truth of Jesus' sonship in the flesh just as clearly as symbolic material points to the truth of his eternal status. Both types of assertion, embedded in the Synoptic Gospels, are articulated clearly and to telling effect in the Epistle to the Hebrews.

For the purposes of our discussion, what is crucial to appreciate is the difference between a circumstantial statement and an historical statement. What shows the truth about Jesus in Hebrews and in the Gospels is *not* any ordered *sequence* of consequential events, but the revelation of divine purpose and salvation within human affairs. Typology, that is, involves a view of past events which sees them as consequential, but not as essentially sequential. Time is not a vital consideration, because what determines one's faith is atemporal: the types of Israel, Jesus in the flesh, and the eternal Christ. Those three fundamental categories of existence are coordinated with one another, but they do not necessitate a sequence of development from year to year. Moreover, they do not involve any claim of causal connection from event to event.

In its assertion of consequence without necessary sequence, typology as developed in Hebrews and in early Christianity remains an ahistorical perspective. Nonetheless, it increasingly involved an emphasis upon Jesus in what Hebrews called "the days of his flesh," and it insisted upon the significance of salvation for people who continued to live in the flesh. The struggle with Gnosticism (discussed in Chapter 6) made that development inevitable, and its clearest representative is Irenaeus, as we have seen.

But for all the daring profundity of Irenaeus' contribution, he did not articulate a theory of what we could call history. The consequence of the Incarnation was absolute, but by definition it did not emerge from any sequence of events which were determined by the terms and conditions of this world. That point is sometimes difficult to grasp for modern readers, because it is generally assumed as a matter of course that Christianity operates within assertions about history.[3] But history speaks of sequence as well as of consequence: from the time of the Gospels until the present, Christian faith indeed speaks of events, but of events which are as non-sequential as they are without precedent. Real time for Irenaeus dissolves the appearances of this world into the prophecies of the past, their fulfillment in Christ, and the totally restored humanity which recapitulation promises. Within such a perspective, history does not even have the significance of a footnote.

On the side of those who were sympathetic with Origen, moreover, the role of history was severely limited. He himself was inclined to see the writings of Moses as an example of *historia* (see *On First Principles* 4.2.6, 8, 9; 4.3.4), a matter for literal reading. The aim of deeper interpretation was to find the allegorical or spiritual meaning which provides insight into the restoration (*apokatastasis*) of all things in Christ, a transformation which can only occur *outside* the terms and conditions of this world.[4] Any limitation to the realm of literal history was for Origen the most dangerous self-deception.

The difference between Irenaeus and Origen is instructive on several levels. Although they both invested what happened to Jesus in the flesh with profound meaning, each understood the proper medium of that meaning characteristically. In the more millenial perspective of Irenaeus, what happened in the case of one person of flesh has consequence for all people of flesh, and *vice versa*. In the more philosophical mode of Origen, Jesus' flesh is important as the occasion to reveal the divine nature of the spiritual body, a reality which only the restoration of all things will manifest fully.

The difference between the *recapitulatio* of Irenaeus and the *apokatastasis* of Origen is more than a matter of nomenclature. It also reflects the dividing line between millenial and philosophical views of eschatological transformation, and distinctive assessments of the value of the flesh. Because history is also a matter of what happens to flesh and blood, for Irenaeus the speculations of theology may take on an almost historical form, while for Origen history only provides a possible occasion for philosophical reflection.

Yet for Irenaeus as for Origen, the appropriate interests of theology are only quasi-historical. Flesh is the medium of revelation in Irenaeus, while it is related to revelation in Origen. Those are two ways of recognizing the flesh of Jesus and one's own flesh as consequential, but not as sequential. Neither writer imagines history as being started and then methodically pushed along by God in order to lead up to the kingdom of heaven. During the twentieth century, some Christians of a liberal caste of mind adhered to a movement called "the social Gospel," and that movement did (and does among its current successors) invoke the pattern of a linear line of progress in divine revelation.[5]

But in Classical Christianity there could be no such simplistic picture of the unfolding of history, because there was not even an agreement that history existed as a category of divine action. God had given flesh consequence: that followed immediately from any understanding of the Incarnation, whether along the lines of an Irenaeus or an Origen. But the consequentiality of flesh had been donated by God himself in the case of Jesus. Flesh was not held to have an inherent value, such that one human event leading to another could produce revelation. Sequence in early Christianity proved to be a much more elusive aspect of history than consequence.

The discovery of the significance of historical sequence within Christianity was perhaps the most radical inheritance of the Constantinian settlement. In most of the areas of its life, the Church had at least some slight preparation for the transformations which were involved. In politics, Christians had no experience of leadership, but they had already thought through the relationship between secular power and eternal salvation. In their values, they had faced up to the question of the goods of this world, so that they could react to the blandishments of the empire with the thriving movements of asceticism which multiplied from the fourth century onward. Teleologically, whatever grandeur the Empire might offer could only pale into insignificance in comparison with the glory which was to come. But history – specifically, history as a *sequence* of events – could scarcely be ignored or slighted, when it seemed actually to validate the claims of the gospel. There was a before Constantine and an after Constantine in a way that there has not been a before and after Marcus Aurelius, or even Augustus. Something happened which demanded a sequential explanation.

EUSEBIUS OF CAESAREA (260–340)

That explanation, and the beginning of Christian history, came with Eusebius (260–340), bishop of Caesarea. Through Pamphilus, his teacher and model, Eusebius had been deeply influenced by the thought of Origen. So, before there was a consciously Christian history, there was an irony of history: from the least historical perspective there was provided the first comprehensively historical account of the meaning of Christ. His prominence in the ecumenical Church at various councils from Nicea onward, as well as his friendship with Constantine, go a long way towards explaining why Eusebius should have made the contribution which makes him the Herodotus of ecclesiastical history.

As he attempted to express the startling breakthrough under

Constantine, Eusebius portrayed the new Emperor as chosen by God himself. The most famous result of his meditation on the significance of the new order is his *History of the Church*, a vitally important document which takes up the Christian story from the time of Christ. The settlement under Constantine is his goal, however, and his portrayal of the Emperor is perhaps most vividly conveyed in his *Praise of Constantine*. After speaking of Christ as the Word of God which holds dominion over the whole world, Eusebius goes on to make a comparison with Constantine:

> Our Emperor, beloved of God, bearing a kind of image of the supreme rule as it were in imitation of the greater, directs the course of all things upon earth.

> (*Praise of Constantine* 1.6)

Here the old Stoic idea of the rule of the Emperor as commensurate with the divine rule is provided with a new substance: the Emperor who obeys Christ himself imitates Christ's glory. Eusebius was inclined to describe himself as moderately capable,[6] and that may be an accurate assessment of him as a theologian and historian. But as a political theorist, he is one of the most influential thinkers in the West. He provided the basis upon which the Roman Empire could be presented as the Holy Roman Empire, and the grounds for claiming the divine right of rulers. At the same time, his reference to the conditional nature of those rights, as dependent upon the imitation of Christ, has provided a basis upon which political revolution may be encouraged on religious grounds.

Part of Eusebius' argument was that Constantine restored the united form of the Empire which had been the ideal of Augustus.[7] After a preface which sets out Christ's divine and human natures, Eusebius carefully places Christ's birth during Augustus' reign, after the subjugation of Egypt (*History of the Church* 1.5). The pairing of Augustus and Christ, Christ and Constantine is therefore symmetrical, and defines the scope of the work. The result is to present a theologically structured political history.

The extent of that history is determined by its political horizon, much as in the case of Eusebius' predecessors in classical history. Whether we think of Herodotus in his explanation of the Persian War, or of Thucydides in the case of the Peloponnesian War, the impetus of writing history seems to be the experience of political change and dislocation. The scope of such work would be extended by such writers as Polybius (the apologist for Rome) and Josephus (the apologist for Judaism), but the desire to learn from the past in the effort to construct a more politically viable present is evident throughout.

Most readers of Eusebius feel uncomfortable with his apology for Constantine. Although the form is political history, the substance seems embarrassingly like flattery. How could Eusebius so thoroughly fail to be critical, whether as historian or as theologian? As an historian, he knew that kings and their flatterers were transient; as a theologian in the line of Origen, he knew that perfection eluded human flesh. The key to this riddle lies in Eusebius' conviction that Christ was at work in Constantine's conversion:

> From that time on a day bright and radiant, with no cloud over-shadowing it, shone down with shafts of heavenly light on the churches of Christ throughout the world, nor was there any reluctance to grant even those outside our community the enjoyment, if not of equal blessings, at least of an effluence from and a share in the things that God had bestowed on us.
>
> (*History of the Church* 10.1)

The sharp change from persecution and all it involved was as disorienting for Eusebius as the Peloponnesian War had been to Thucydides, and an explanation was demanded. In that explanation, ecclesiastical history was born: that is, not simply the anecdotes of experience, but a rational account of God's activity within human events. The sequence of flesh met the consequence of flesh, and history was the offspring.

The intervention in the case of Constantine and his colleague Licinius (who at first reigned with Constantine) was nothing less than the appointed plan of God within a definite sequence of events. Eusebius reminds the reader of the terrible tortures Christians had experienced, and then proceeds:

> But once again the Angel of the great counsel, God's great Commander-in-Chief, after the thoroughgoing training through which the greatest soldiers in his kingdom gave proof by their patience and endurance in all trials, appeared suddenly and thereby swept all that was hostile and inimical into oblivion and nothingness, so that its very existence was forgotten. But all that was near and dear to Him He advanced beyond glory in the sight of all, not men only but the heavenly powers as well – sun, moon, and stars, and the entire heaven and earth.
>
> (*History of the Church* 10.4)

Only the language of apocalypse, of the sequenced revelation of God himself in Christ, can explain to Eusebius' satisfaction how the former agony can so quickly have been transformed into festivity. In Constantine, the promised future had begun, and there was no room for a return to the past.

The picture which Eusebius draws of the contemporary scene (after the narrative of the removal of Licinius) might have been drawn from an apocalyptic work in Hellenistic dress:

> Men had now lost all fear of their former oppressors; day after day they kept dazzling festival; light was everywhere, and men who once dared not look up greeted each other with smiling faces and shining eyes. They danced and sang in city and country alike, giving honor first to God our Sovereign Lord, as they had been instructed, and then to the pious Emperor with his sons, so dear to God.
>
> (*History of the Church* 10.9)

History for Eusebius was not just an account of the past, it was an apocalypse in reverse. His account was designed to set out the sequence of events which brought about the dawn of a new age.

Long before Eusebius, Origen had written that Rome would prosper better than even the children of Israel had by worshiping the true God (*Against Celsus* 8.69). For Origen, the argument was hypothetical; for Eusebius, it had become a reality. The new unity of the Empire, under God, in Christ, and through the piety of the Emperor himself, constituted for Eusebius a divine polity (*politeia* or *politeuma*), literally a breath away from paradise. It is as if the millenarianism of Justin and Irenaeus had been made the prelude to the spiritual transformation of Clement and Origen. *Recapitulatio* contributed the sequence, and *apokatastasis* represented the aim, of Eusebius' theology of history.

AUGUSTINE OF HIPPO (354–430)

If Christian history was born under the pressure of success, its baptism of fire was the experience of an unimaginable failure. In 410 CE, Alaric sacked the city of Rome itself. That event was a stunning blow to the Empire generally, but it was a double blow to Latin Christianity. First, the pillage occurred while the Empire was Christian; two centuries before, Tertullian had argued that idolatry brought about disaster (see *Apologeticus* 41.1), and now Christianity could be said to do so. Second, Latin Christianity – especially in North Africa – had been particularly attracted to a millenarian eschatology. How could one explain that the triumphant end of history, announced by Eusebius and his followers, seemed to be reversed by the Visigoths?

The explanation of that dilemma occupied Augustine in his *City of God*, a tremendous work of twenty-three books, written between 413 and 426. From the outset he sounds his theme, that the City of God is an eternal city which exists in the midst of the city of men; those two cities are both mixed and at odds in this world, but they are to be separated by the final judgment (*City of God* 1.1). That essentially simple thesis is sustained through an account of Roman religion and Hellenistic philosophy, including Augustine's critical appreciation of Plato (books 1–10).

In the central section of his work, Augustine sets out his case within a discussion of truly global history, from the story of the creation in Genesis. From the fall of the angels, which Augustine associates with the separation of light and darkness in Gen. 1:4, he speaks of the striving between good and evil. But the distinction between those two is involved with the will of certain angels, not with any intrinsic wickedness (*City of God* 11.33). People, too, are disordered in their desire, rather than in their creation by God (*City of God* 12.8).

The difference between the will God intends for his creatures and the will they actually evince attests the freedom involved in divine creation. But the effect of perverted will, whether angelic or human, is to establish two antithetical regimes:

> So two loves have constituted two cities – the earthly is formed by love of self even to contempt of God, the heavenly by love of God even to contempt of self. For the one glories in herself, the other in the Lord. The one seeks glory from man; for the other God, the witness of the conscience, is the greatest glory. . . . In the one the lust for power prevails, both in her own rulers and in the nations she subdues; in the other all serve each other in charity, governors by taking thought for all and subjects by obeying.
>
> (*City of God* 14.28)

By book 18, Augustine arrives at his own time, and repeats that the two cities "alike enjoy temporal goods or suffer temporal ills, but differ in faith, in hope, in love, until they be separated by the final judgment and each receive its end, of which there is no end" (*City of God* 18.54).

That commits Augustine to speak of eschatological issues, which he does until the end of the work as a whole. It is in his discussion of eschatology that Augustine frames classic and orthodox responses to some of the most persistent questions of the Christian theology of his time. He adheres to the expectation of the resurrection of the flesh, not simply of the body (as had been the manner of Origen). In so doing, he refutes the Manichaean philosophy which he accepted prior to his conversion to Christianity. In Manichaeanism, named after a Persian teacher of the third century named Mani, light and darkness are two eternal substances which struggle against one another, and they war over the creation they have both participated in making.[9] As in the case of Gnosticism, on which it was dependent, Manichaeanism counselled a denial of the flesh. By his insistence on the resurrection of the flesh, Augustine revives the strong assertion of the extent of God's embrace of his own creation in the tradition of Irenaeus.

At the same time, Augustine sets a limit on the extent to which one might have recourse to Plato. Augustine had insisted with Plato against the Manichaeans that God was not a material substance, but transcendent. Similarly, evil became in his mind the denial of what proceeds from God (see *Confessions* 5.10.20). When it came to the creation of people, however, Augustine insisted against Platonic thought that no division between soul and flesh could be made (so *City of God* 22.12). Enfleshed humanity was the only genuine humanity, and God in Christ was engaged to raise those who were of the city of God. Moreover, Augustine specifically refuted the contention of Porphyry (and Origen) that cycles of creation could be included within the entire scheme of salvation. For Augustine, the power of the resurrection within the world was already confirmed by the miracles wrought by Christ and his martyrs. He gives the example of the healings connected with the relics of St. Stephen, recently transferred to Hippo (*City of God* 22.8).

Even now, in the power of the Catholic Church, God is represented on earth, and the present, Christian epoch (*Christiana tempora*) corresponds to the millennium promised in Rev. 20 (*City of God* 20.9).[10] This age of dawning power, released in flesh by Jesus and conveyed by the Church, simply awaits the full transition into the City of God, complete with flesh itself. It is interesting that, where Origen could cite a saying of Jesus to confirm his view of the resurrection (see Matt. 22:29–30; Mark 12:24–25; Luke 20:34–36), Augustine has to qualify the same saying:

They will be equal to angels in immortality and happiness, not in flesh, nor indeed in resurrection, which the angels had no need of, since they could not die. So the Lord said that there would be no marriage in the resurrection, not that there would be no women.

(*City of God* 22.18)

In all of this Augustine is straining, although he is usually a straight-forward interpreter of Scripture. But he is wedded to what the Latin confession of "the resurrection of the flesh" implies, and therefore cannot follow Origen's exegesis of a purely spiritual body. There is a double irony here. First, Origen – the sophisticated allegorist – seems much simpler to follow than Augustine, the incomparable preacher. Second, Augustine's discussion of such issues as the fate of foetuses in the resurrection sounds remarkably like the Sadducees' hypothesis which Jesus argues *against* in the relevant passage from the Synoptic Gospels.

Augustine is well aware, as was Origen before him, that Paul speaks of a "spiritual body," and acknowledges that "I suspect that all utterance published concerning it is rash." And yet he can be quite categorical that flesh must be involved somehow: "the spiritual flesh will be subject to spirit, but it will still be flesh, not spirit; just as the carnal spirit was subject to the flesh, but was still spirit, not flesh" (*City of God* 22.21). Such is Augustine's conviction that flesh has become the medium of salvation, now and hereafter. As in the case of Irenaeus, the denial of a thoroughly abstract teaching leads to the assertion of greater literalism than may have been warranted.

In his adherence to a kind of millenarianism and to the resurrection of the flesh in the Latin creed, Augustine is very much a product of North Africa and Italy, where he was active (chiefly as a teacher of rhetoric) prior to his conversion and his return to North Africa. But his *City of God* creates the greater frame, primordial and eschatological, within which history becomes a theological discipline. Here, he argues, is more than a lesson in how to avoid war and create order. And here there is certainly more than the superficial enthusiasm which comes of histories written by the winners. Rather, history for Augustine – and from Augustine – is the interplay of those two forces which determine the existence of every society, every person.

Augustine died in Hippo while the city was actually under siege by the Vandals. His passing, and the passing of his church and his city, was a curious witness to his *Christiana tempora*. But his conception that his history and every history reflected the struggle between the two cities prepared him and the global Church for that, and for much worse. He had turned back to the Eusebian model of history as apocalypse, and he took it even more seriously than Eusebius himself had. No apocalyptic seer ever promised an easy transition to the consuming reign of Christ, and on to that moment when God would be all in all (so 1 Cor. 15:28, a promise which was dear to Augustine). Smooth, unhampered progress is a model of history which only recommends itself to those in the line of Eusebius (and historians since the nineteenth century!). If history is apocalyptic, because the times of the Church are millenial, then our flesh has indeed been blessed, but our history is equally dedicated to struggle.

The struggle, however, is not ultimately between good and evil, but between the love of God and the love of self. That is the key to Augustine's ceaseless, pastoral ministry, as well as to his remarkably broad intellectual horizon. In every time and in every place, there is the possibility that the City of God will be revealed and embraced; now, in the *Christiana tempora*, we at last know its name, and can see the face of that love which would transform us all.

History after Augustine could be painted on canvasses of indeterminate size, because he established the quest to integrate the historical task with philosophical reflection. At the same time, in his *Confessions*, he established the genre of autobiography as an investigation of the dynamics of universal salvation within the life of the individual he knew best, himself. Written large in nations and written small in persons, history attested the outward-working and inward-working power of God, if only one's eyes could see with the love of God, and be freed of the blindness of self-love.

CONCLUSION

Eusebius and Augustine together provided the classical program for Christianity's survival of the decay of the Roman Empire. A political theory of divine right and an historical perspective of the two cities would contribute the matrix for the remains of the Empire in the East and the petty kingdoms in the West to construct successive, variant, sometimes conflicting models of Christ's kingdom of earth. Without reference to those two ideologies, an understanding of the Middle Ages is simply impossible.

The contribution of Eusebius is frequently overlooked, because the "Constantinian triumphalism" of which he was the chronicler has long been out of fashion, whether within the Church or without. But a commitment to a monarch who is Christ's regent in fact survived both the Reformation and the Renaissance; only the age of the Enlightenment saw it superseded. Even that supersession involved a cognate commitment: to the idea that nationally constituted people could and should assert their inherent rights, as "endowed by their Creator," in the words of the Declaration of Independence.

Two factors especially have tended to obscure the religious grounds of political thought. First, the Enlightenment represented an appeal to universal reason apart from any engagement of faith. In the light of events since the eighteenth century, that appeal – with its naive corollary that people act out of enlightened self-interest – has lost plausibility. The second factor is related to the first. The Soviet Union represented what was perceived as a threat to the "West" in essentially secular terms. That Cold War (which indeed involved the resources of a major war) resulted in the elevation of the ideologies of "Capitalism" and "Communism" to the realm of religious commitment. Now that the Soviet Union is a thing of the past, it is obvious that the West's "Capitalism" was no purer than the East's "Communism," and that neither constitutes a comprehensive account of the way of life, of social order, or of the significance of the world in the manner of religion. Discussion of government along explicitly religious lines – particularly among Christians – may be expected to increase for the foreseeable future.

Augustine's influence is more widely recognized than Eusebius', and it is unquestionably deeper. Global history and personal history have perennially been seen as revelatory; echoes of the *City of God* and the *Confessions* are heard in books, seen in movies, resonant in political arguments and personal disclosures. It may not be too much to say that with Augustine the human being in historical experience was invented. And he nuanced what he meant by history; its time was for him not atomistic segments. Time for Augustine was rather our remembrance of the past, our expectation for the future, our attention in the present (see *Confessions* 11). History, in today's jargon, was "constructed" in his understanding.

Considerable attention has been given this century to the eclipse of the view of history as objective events, the story of what "really happened." Facts, to be sure, remain at the end of this debate: there are inferences which can be verified, and there are inferences which cannot be verified. But the arrangement of verifiable data into a sequenced account, and the determination of the scope of the inquiry, those can not be decided by anything approaching an objective standard.[11]

Augustine provides self-conscious answers to the questions of the sequence (including the scope) and the consequence of history. And he shows how confronting the past belongs to the human task, personal and collective, of living in the present and fashioning a future. He also, in his emphatic reference to the two cities, allows for the disruption of history's consequence and sequence. In that denial of simple progress, Augustine demonstrates that the struggle between flesh and spirit (and therefore between Irenaeus and Origen) is far from over.

GLOSSARY

Aggadah, the norms of belief, is the word for narrative "telling," and refers to the corpus of the wise sayings, stories, doctrine, and scriptural exegesis that all together sets forth the theology of Rabbinic Judaism. *See* Halakhah.

The **Amoraim** are the authorities of the two Talmuds: the Talmud of the Land of Israel, *ca.* 400 CE and the Talmud of Babylonia, *ca.* 600 CE. They provided the commentary to the Mishnah, *ca.* 200 CE, the philosophical law code that marked the beginning of the writing down of the Oral Torah. *See* Tannaim.

Antinomies are two statements which are in contradiction to one another, although each has a considerable claim to truth. The aim of philosophical analysis is to resolve that contradiction, or to understand why it can not be resolved.

An **Apocalypse** is a revelation (*apokalupsis* in Greek) which relates the last things in human history leading up to and including the end. The revelation is usually attributed to a heavenly agent and involves a calendar and sequence of events which relates present hardship to the definitive triumph which is to come.

Apollo was the Greek god of light, the arts, and divination, and was famously represented at Delphi by the Pythian oracle.

Catholic Christianity is, as has been said since the second century, faith "through the whole" (*kath' holu* in Greek) of the Church. The point is that the faith which is catholic is accepted by the Church as such, and does not involve purely local or speculative beliefs.

Clement of Alexandria offered instruction to Christians in that great city until 202 CE, when a persecution was pursued under the Emperor Septimus Severus. Clement developed a comprehensive Christian philosophy which related the gospel to the divine Logos, the Word of God by which the world was created and through which human beings may share God's reason. In his teaching, he stressed that the Logos addressed our passions as well as our intellect, in contrast to the Gnosticism which was also popular in Alexandria.

The **Cross** in Christian theology is not only the place of Jesus' execution, but the point of intersection between what God reveals to the world and what people do in order to resist the love of God. Especially in the thought of St. Paul, the cross stands for the gospel as a whole in its relationship to the world.

Delphi is on the southern slope of Mount Parnassus in Greece, and was the site where it was said Apollo had killed the great snake (the *python*); the priestess who revealed the wisdom of Apollo there was called the Pythian oracle.

Dialectic is the oppositional method of argument, in which one seeks truth by setting up a proposition over and against an opposing statement, and by dialogue or debate seeks to evaluate the strengths or weaknesses of the two.

Dionysus was god of the wine in Greece, and also of death and rebirth. Dionysian rites were designed to initiate followers into the Mysteries of his death and rebirth, so that they might benefit from his power.

Ethics of the Fathers, a.k.a. Pirqé Abot, a compendium of wise sayings appended to the Mishnah and attributed to the sages of the Oral Torah from Moses through principal figures in the generation after the closure of the Mishnah in *ca.* 200 CE, hence to be dated at *ca.* 250 CE.

The **Fathers of the Church** are the classic teachers of Christianity between the second century and the eighth century. They are so designated because any catholic "Father" of that period is held within Christianity to be a reliable guide in regard to the faith, even if some aspects of his teaching are not currently accepted.

Gnosticism is the theological insistence, which thrived from the second century until the fifth century in many different forms, that as human beings our only hope for insight into the divine and salvation lies in the knowledge (*gnosis* in Greek). The knowledge involved, however, is less what can be learned than a special disclosure which God grants to a select few.

Haggadah, the narrative that is read at the Passover celebration or seder.

Halakhah, the norms of behavior, the laws and rules of every day life that define what the faithful Israelite is expected to do or to refrain from doing. The principal source of the halakhah for the first centuries CE is the Mishnah and its commentaries, the two Talmuds, as well as the exegesis of the legal passages of Exodus, Leviticus, Numbers, and Deuteronomy, that is set forth in related exegetical compilations.

Logos or Word, within Christian theology, is God's ordering principle and design in the creation of the world. It is responsible for the maintenance of that world within a pattern which human reason is capable of apprehending. The capacity to appreciate the Word of God implies that God's own reason is accessible to us: that divine reason is Jesus Christ.

Manichaeanism derives from the Persian teacher Mani from the third century CE. The teaching holds that light and darkness are two eternal principles which war against one another, and struggle for supremacy in this world, which they have both participated in making. For Mani, only knowledge of the light, beyond this world, can offer salvation.

A **Metonym** is a word used in a transferred sense, such that the part may express the whole, or the cause may express the complete result.

Midrash is the exegesis of Scripture. For Rabbinic Judaism there are three main types of compilations of Midrash, line by line readings of phrases and clauses; systematic compositions formed to demonstrate diverse propositions through scriptural exegesis; and entire compilations devoted to a group of cogent propositions.

The **Mishnah**, *ca.* 200 CE, is a law code set forth on philosophical principles of natural history, so organized and presented as to present a hierarchical ordering of matters of concern to the holy life of Israel, God's people. It consists of 530 chapters, set forth as sixty-two topical expositions called tractates, all together divided into six divisions, dealing with the sanctification of Israel's life in agriculture, the rhythm of the week, the lunar month, and the year, the life of the family, the civil order (including political institutions), the holy cult in the Temple in Jerusalem, and the protection thereof from levitical uncleanness.

Millenarianism is the apocalyptic teaching that the followers of Christ will reign with him for one thousand years (a millennium), after which time there will be a last conflict with the devil and the final judgment (see Revelation 20).

Persephone in Greek mythology was the daughter of Zeus and Demeter. In one of the most famous Mysteries, the initiate could identify with her, as she was kidnapped and taken to the underworld, whence she escaped in the spring.

Platonism, by our period, focuses on the theory that the world which we perceive reflects an ideal reality. What can be experienced are types – in the sense of impresses – of a primordial truth.

Progressive, according to the meaning of the word used in this volume, refers to the development of a principle or truth through human experience and history, such that one is in a better position to evaluate the whole at the end of the development than at any earlier point. A progressive understanding is therefore the opposite of an originalist reading, which takes the beginning point of an experience or a history as the measure of the whole.

The **Pseudepigrapha** is the body of literature read widely within early Christianity and Judaism as Scripture, yet never widely enough accepted to become canonical. Pseudepigraphic works are typically attributed to a biblical author, and purport to reveal some hidden aspect of Judaism or Christianity, sometimes of an apocalyptic nature.

A **Sage** is a master of the Torah, written and oral, set forth by God to Moses at Sinai and handed on in a chain formed from master through disciple, beginning with God and Moses, from the revelation at Sinai to the age of the Mishnah and the Talmud through a process of oral formulation and oral transmission.

Syncretism refers to a culture in which the elements of many diverse cultures are mixed together, such as to create the possibility of new religions and philosophies.

Stoicism teaches that a single, divine reason governs both nature and human affairs. Although Stoicism began in Greece (and is named after the portico, the *stoa*, in Athens where the founding discussions began), it became the most popular philosophy in Rome, where it was embraced by Emperor Marcus Aurelius during the second century CE.

A **System of religion** sets forth an encompassing account of the social order that God initiates, involving a theory of a way of life, or ethics, a world view or ethics, and of the social group formed by those who live in accord with the one and explain who they are in accord with the other. A system of religion commonly organizes itself around a set of compelling questions and provides for the faithful self-evidently valid answers to those questions. A system of religion always begins with a social group and addresses itself to that group.

The **Talmud** is a class of ancient Rabbinic Judaic exegetical writings serving the Mishnah, of which there are two, the Talmud of the Land of Israel, *ca.* 400 CE, and the Talmud of Babylonia, *ca.* 600 CE. Each Talmud is made up of two components, the Mishnah itself, and the commentary thereto, which may be called "the Gemara" or simply "the Talmud." The Talmud of the Land of Israel treats thirty tractates of the Mishnah, and the Talmud of Babylonia, thirty-seven. Of the Mishnah's six divisions, the Talmud of the Land of Israel deals with the first four, and the one of Babylonia, the second through the fifth. So there are two Talmudic commentaries to the second, third, and fourth divisions of the Mishnah.

The **Tannaim** are the authorities of the Mishnah and related writings, *ca.* 50 BCE through 200 CE. These are the sages who shaped the first of the two components of the Talmuds of the Land of Israel and of Babylonia, *ca.* 400 and 600, respectively. *See* Amoraim.

The **Targumim** are paraphrases of the Hebrew Bible in the Aramaic language. Aramaic became the principal language of Judaism during the fifth century BCE, which necessitated a translation (*targum* in Aramaic) of the Bible into that language. The actual documents which represent the Targumim date from the third century until the eighth century CE, although some of their traditions are earlier than that and many of their glosses are later than that.

Tertullian was a prominent teacher of Catholic Christianity until around the year 207 CE, when he converted to the movement called Montanism. Montanus had taught that he himself was a vessel of the Holy Spirit, and that his followers might become so, if they were suitably prepared. Tertullian had been attracted to that sort of perfectionism even before his conversion, and represents the keen consciousness of the importance of martyrdom within the early Church.

Torah: God's self-manifestation and revelation of his will through Moses to holy Israel, the people called to Sinai to encounter that self-manifestation and to accept and adopt that revelation. In Rabbinic Judaism the Torah is set forth in two media, the one in writing, the other through oral formulation and oral transmission. The former part of the Torah, called the Written Torah, corresponds in most particulars to the Protestant Old Testament (omitting the Apocrypha and Pseudepigrapha, which have no standing in Rabbinic Judaism). The latter part of the Torah, called the Oral Torah or the Torah that is memorized, ultimately was transcribed in the formulation of "our sages of blessed memory," the Tannaim and Amoraim who produced the Rabbinic documents of late antiquity.

The **Tosefta** is a collection of Tannaite teachings correlative to the Mishnah, produced about a half-century after the closure of the Mishnah and organized in response to the Mishnah's modes of organization. It contains three types of material: citation and gloss of the Mishnah; compositions that complement the Mishnah's rules but do not cite the Mishnah's laws verbatim; and compositions that stand autonomous of the Mishnah's laws altogether, though harmonious in general with those laws. About a third of the Tosefta consists of Mishnah-citation and gloss; about half complements to the Mishnah, and about a sixth free-standing supplements to the Mishnah. The Tosefta organizes its materials in that same order: Mishnah-citation, Mishnah-complement, then Mishnah-supplement.

The **Trinity** analyzes the essence of God, and finds that God is one through all eternity, and at the same time asserts that God is known in three aspects. Father, Son, and Holy Spirit, are the triad within which all manifestations of God may be known, and the relationships by which God functions in respect of himself.

NOTES

PREFACE

1 G. E. R. Lloyd, (1970) *Early Greek Science. Thales to Aristotle* (New York: W. W. Norton & Co.), pp. 11–12.
2 The Jewish philosopher of Alexandria, Philo, wrote in Greek and in no way spoke to the Judaic sages of the Land of Israel.
3 G. E. R. Lloyd, (1970) *Early Greek Science Thales to Aristotle* (New York: W. W. Norton & Co.), p. 15.
4 Here we follow the model of the inestimable G. E. R. Lloyd, (1966) *Polarity and Analogy. Two Types of Argumentation in Early Greek Thought* (Cambridge: Cambridge University Press), pp. 6–7.

CHAPTER 1 CONFRONTING CONFLICT IN THE MISNAH

1 I have catalogued them all in *The Philosophical Mishnah* (1989) I. *The Initial Probe* II. *The Tractates' Agenda. From Abodah Zarah to Moed Qatan* III. *The Tractates' Agenda. From Nazir to Zebahim* IV. The Repertoire (Atlanta: Scholars Press for Brown Judaic Studies). The results are then set forth systematically in *Judaism as Philosophy. The Method and Message of the Mishnah* (1991) (Columbia: University of South Carolina Press).
2 Or any Israelite in the Holy Land who intended to observe the rules of cultic cleanness even outside of the cult and for other than hieratic purposes. That matter does not concern us here.
3 But in fact, much assigned to the two Houses takes for granted legal principles otherwise attested only in the mouths of second-century authorities. Not only so, but the attributions serve as formalities, with opinions assigned to the named authorities systematically revised as logic requires. So we need not be detained by trivial questions of historicity.
4 G. Vermes, *The Dead Sea Scrolls in English* (1962) (Harmondsworth: Penguin Books).
5 Ibid., p. 83.
6 Ibid., p. 112.
7 Deut. 22:5, 6, 8, 9, 12.

8 Translation: *The Oxford Annotated Bible with the Apocrypha. Revised Standard Version.* (1965) Edited by Herbert G. May and Bruce M. Metzger (New York: Oxford University Press), pp. 419–420.

9 I do not concur in that allegation as to the "genre" of the Mishnah, but once more introduce it for the sake of argument. In fact a single document cannot define, or constitute, a genre at all. And the Mishnah's singularity is its indicative trait in the Israelite context.

10 On the relationship of Qumran and Rabbinic Sabbath law, see Lawrence H. Schiffman (1975) *The Halakhah at Qumran* (E. J. Brill: Leiden).

11 We make provision for a possible exception in the case of Job, but supernatural debate and debate between men are surely to be classified differently.

12 The dispute in the Midrash-compilations must be addressed in its own terms. But when it comes to debates and extended dialogues, the Gemaras of the two Talmuds stand by themselves even when compared with the later Midrash-compilations, beyond Sifra.

13 Lloyd, *Early Greek Science*, p. 8.

14 That is not to argue for one minute that our sages studied philosophy before, during, or after their yeshiva-years (to speak anachronistically). Historicistic questions of origins, theories of influence and borrowing – these presuppose traits of culture and its formation and diffusion that require attention in their own terms. Why anyone should find surprising in the age of Neo-Platonism that our sages should produce a work such as the Mishnah, congruent in method and intent to neo-Platonic writing (as I show in *Judaism as Philosophy*), seems to me also to require an explanation. There I argue that comparison and contrast by definition acknowledge no boundaries of culture or historical context. By rights and by simple logic we can compare and contrast anything that falls into the same classification with anything else in that same classification. Since people in widely separated places may and often do come to the same conclusions about the same things, we commit no act of violence against common sense by invoking in this context the names of Aristotle as to method, and Plato and Middle Platonism and particularly the Neo-Platonism that came to full expression only later on in the writings of Plotinus as to proposition. What we seek, as a matter of fact, is nothing more than the *classification*, as philosophy, of the Mishnah's method and message. I maintain that that message and method exhibit congruence with philosophies of the same kind, that is, philosophies that, whole or in part, ask the same types of questions and pursue the same means for answering them. To the comparison of structures of thought historical questions of time and circumstance prove monumentally irrelevant.

15 In Chapter 3, we proceed from the dispute and debate to the dialectical argument, a separate matter altogether.

16 This is fully spelled out in G. E. R. Lloyd (1966) *Polarity and Analogy. Two Types of Argumentation in Early Greek Thought* (Cambridge: Cambridge University Press).

17 Lloyd, *Early Greek Science* pp. 433–434.

18 Lloyd, pp. 418–419.

CHAPTER 2 CONFRONTING CONFLICT IN THE LETTERS OF PAUL

1 God's name as "Father" itself features in the Targumim, early Judaic, liturgical prayers, and the Pseudepigrapha. Cf. Chilton, "God as Father in the Targumim, non-canonical literatures of Judaism and Christianity, and Matthew," *The Pseudepigrapha and the New Testament: Comparative Studies* (1993) (ed. J. H. Charlesworth and C. A. Evans) (Sheffield: JSOT), pp. 151–169.

2 By way of contrast, see 1 Cor. 1:4–9. In that Paul is vociferous in his attack on some practices in Corinth, the omission of any such preamble in Galatians is all the more striking.

3 See Jerome H. Neyrey, (1990) *Paul, in Other Words. A Cultural Reading of His Letters* (Louisville: Westminster).

4 Richard B. Hays, (1989) *Echoes of Scripture in the Letters of Paul* (New Haven: Yale) p. 114.

5 Ibid.

6 See, for example, John G. Lodge, (1996) *Romans 9–11. A Reader-Response Analysis*: International Studies in Formative Christianity and Judaism 6 (Atlanta: Scholars), for a considered appraisal of prominent theories of interpretation.

7 Richard B. Hays, (1989) *Echoes of Scripture in the Letters of Paul* (New Haven: Yale), p. 117.

8 Jerone H. Neyrey, (1990) *Paul, in Other Words. A Cultural Reading of His Letters* (Louisville: Westminster), p. 191.

9 That argument is not to be detailed here, since it features prominently in Chilton and Neusner, (1995) *Judaism in the New Testament. Practices and Beliefs* (London: Routledge) pp. 62–71.

10 Ibid., pp. 98–128

11 As we have argued at some length in ibid., 58–103.

12 The tendency that Philo had to contend with was not limited to Alexandria: see Friedrich Wilhelm Horn, (1996) "Der Verzicht auf die Beschneidung im frühen Christentum", *New Testament Studies* 42 pp. 470–505.

13 In her fine study, *The Covenant in Judaism and Paul. A Study of Ritual Boundaries as Identity Markers*, Arbeiten zur Geschichte des Antiken Judentums und des Urchristentums XXVII (Leiden: E. J. Brill, 1995), pp. 323–324.

14 Ibid., pp. 239–249.

15 For a discussion of its significance, see J. A. Ziesler, (1990) *Pauline Christianity:* The Oxford Bible Series (Oxford: Oxford University Press), pp. 49–72.

16 Chilton and Neusner, (1995) *Judaism in the New Testament. Practices and Beliefs* (London: Routledge), p. 184. For the analysis overall, see pp. 181–188.

17 See Heb. 8:1–6. Hebrews' usage of the language of typology is quite complex, although the underlying conception is fairly simple.

18 See C. K. Barrett (1962), *From First Adam to Last. A Study in Pauline Theology* (New York: Scribner's), p. 50.

19 See Henry Chadwick, (1993) *The Early Church* (London: Penguin), pp. 29, 74–79.

20 R. M. Grant, (1963) *A Short History of the Interpretation of the Bible* (New York: Macmillan), p. 66.
21 For a discussion of the Aqedah and related matters, see Chilton, (1986) *Targumic Approaches to the Gospels. Essays in the Mutual Definition of Judaism and Christianity:* Studies in Judaism (Lanham and London: University Press of America).

CHAPTER 3 CONDUCTING DIALECTICAL ARGUMENT IN THE TALMUD

1 Cited by C. D. Reeve, *Practices of Reason. Aristotle's Nicomachean Ethics*, p. 34. The commas are Professor Neusner's own; Reeve gives the sentence without them.
2 As noted in the Preface, we plan a separate work on authority in nascent Christianity and formative Judaism.
3 Dialectical arguments occur in Sifra and the Talmud of the Land of Israel, *c.* 350 and 400 respectively, but in no other document of the Rabbinic canon. Only in the Talmud of Babylonia do we find an ample repertoire of authentic dialectics.
4 Robin Smith, "Logic" in J. Barnes (ed) *Cambridge Companion to Aristotle*, p. 60.
5 I have classified the arguments of the Talmud of Babylonia and identified the authentically dialectical ones, in *Talmudic Dialectics: Types and Form* (1995) (Atlanta: Scholars Press for South Florida Studies in the History of Judaism). I. *Introduction. Tractate Berakhot and the Divisions of Appointed Times and Women.* II. *The Divisions of Damages and Holy Things and Tractate Niddah.*
6 Robin Smith, "Logic" in J. Barnes (ed) *Cambridge Companion to Aristotle*, pp. 58–60.
7 Ibid., pp. 60–61. I do not think we can persuasively compare and contrast the forms of argument set forth in the Topics, where Aristotle sets forth rules "for discovering premises from which to deduce a given conclusion. They rest on a classification of conclusions according to form; each gives premise-forms from which a given form of conclusion can be deduced . . . . Overall, the dialectical method of the Topics requires the joint application of the "locations" and the inventories of opinions. To find my argument, I first look up a location appropriate to my desired conclusion and use it to discover premises that would be useful; then I consult the relevant inventory of opinions to see if those premises are found there. If they are, I have my argument; all that remains is to cast it into the form of questions and present them to my opponent. . . ."
8 For an equivalent exercise of hermeneutics of a contentious order, we look in vain among the other law codes and commentaries of antiquity, which tend to a certain blandness. For the Zoroastrian counterpart, see Neusner, (1993) *Judaism and Zoroastrianism at the Dusk of Late Antiquity. How Two Ancient Faiths Wrote Down Their Great Traditions* (Atlanta: Scholars Press for South Florida Studies in the History of Judaism).
9 In the Talmud of Babylonia, statements bearing the signal, TNY, in its various forms, ordinarily bear the names of authorities who also occur in the

Mishnah; or who are credited with the compilation of Mishnah-sayings, e.g., a Tosefta-compilation, such as Hiyya or Bar Qappara. But in the Talmud of the Land of Israel, the same convention does not prevail, and TNY sayings may routinely occur in the names of authorities who elsewhere occur only with figures much later than the time of the closure of the Mishnah. Whatever the intent of TNY in the Bavli, therefore, the meaning of the signal in the Yerushalmi cannot be the same. It is generally supposed that TNY in the Bavli means a teaching out of Tannaite times. But in the Yerushalmi indifference to chronology, indicated by name associations, then bears a different meaning. There, it follows, TNY signals a status as to authority, not as to origin.

10 A single exception proves the rule. A few sages were employed by the Jewish civil administration of Babylonia, a state-recognized agency called the exilarchate. The exilarchate is represented in the Rabbinic sources as an independent authority over the Jews, and not as a corporate body of sages itself. A few sages, however, are represented as employed by (part of the "household" of) the exilarch. But stories about those few, while acknowledging their political standing, never represent the exilarch's sages as employing power rather than persuasion of a reasoned sort. The pertinent stories are collected in Neusner, (1965–70) *History of the Jews in Babylonia*, Leiden: E. J. Brill, vols. I–V. Chapter 2 of each of the volumes, II–V, is devoted to the exilarchate.

CHAPTER 4 CONDUCTING DIALECTICAL ARGUMENT IN ORIGEN

1 Ethelbert Stauffer has shown that the practice is related to the Judaic custom of prayer and sacrifice on behalf of the dead. See especially 2 Mac. 12:39–45 and Stauffer (1955) (trans. J. Marsh), *New Testament Theology* (New York: Macmillan) p. 299 n. 544.

2 See Jean Daniélou, (1955) *Origen* (trans. W. Mitchell), (New York: Sheed and Ward), p. 13.

3 For a discussion of modalism, and of Origen's crucial place in the development of the Trinity, see J. N. D. Kelly, (1958) *Early Christian Doctrines* (New York: Harper and Row), pp. 109–137.

CHAPTER 5 ARGUMENTS FROM NATURAL HISTORY IN THE MISNAH AND IN LEVITICUS RABBAH

1 That assessment can scarcely be squared with the inconsequential role assigned to the monarchy, but it does accord with the representation of the king and queen as humbly seeking sages' approval (a picture Josephus draws for historic time as well). Within the larger politics, therefore, the king serves to deliver the systemic message: the State, embodied by the king, enjoys full sovereignty, and the sages run the State. Citing verses of Scripture and underlining that the king is superior to the high priest but inferior to the

Torah, which he must obey, reveals this important fact even while it is not made articulate: the king obeys the sages, who are the masters of the Torah.

2 Joseph Owens, (1959) *A History of Ancient Western Philosophy* (New York: Appleton, Century, Crofts Inc.), p. 340.

3 I expand on this point in the Appendix.

CHAPTER 6 ARGUMENTS FROM NATURE: IRENAEUS

1 For a recent and succinct discussion, see S. J. Haferman, (1993) "Corinthians, Letters to the," *Dictionary of Paul and His Letters* (eds G. F. Hawthorne and R. P. Martin) (Downers Grove: InterVarsity).

2 That contrast of light and darkness, in turn, manifests the influence of Zoroastrianism upon Judaism, but that is an entirely separate topic.

3 See George W. MacRae's presentation in *The Nag Hammadi Library* (1978) (ed. J. M. Robinson) (San Francisco: Harper and Row).

4 See Stephen Benko, (1986) *Pagan Rome and the Early Christians* (Bloomington: Indiana University Press); see especially "The Charges of Immorality and Cannibalism," pp. 54–78.

5 See Henry George Liddell and Robert Scott, (1901) *A Greek-English Lexicon* (Oxford: Clarendon), p. 724.

6 See *Against Heresies* 4.33.7. For a discussion of Irenaeus's theology of the Church, see Gustaf Wingren, (1959) *Man and the Incarnation* (Edinburgh: Oliver and Boyd), pp. 147–180.

7 See ibid., 3.9.8.

8 See J. N. D. Kelly, (1949) *Early Christian Creeds* (New York: Longmans, Green), pp. 163–166. As he conclusively shows, the creeds developed over centuries, and there was considerable local variation. Our citation of the Apostles' Creed in its traditional form is intended as a point of departure, rather than as a claim for its originality.

9 H. Chadwick, *The Early Church* (1993) (London: Penguin) p. 80.

10 For a discussion of that issue, see M. Widman, "Irenäus und seine theologische Väter," *Zeitschrift für Theologie und Kirche* 54 (1957), pp. 155–166 and Jean Daniélou and Henri Marrou (1964), *The Christian Centuries. I: The First Six Hundred Years* (New York: McGraw-Hill), p. 112.

11 Lloyd G. Patterson, (1967) *God and History in Early Christian Thought: Studies in Patristic Thought* (New York: Seabury), p. 45.

12 See J. Daniélou and H. Marrou, (1964), *The Christian Centuries. I: The First Six Hundred Years* (New York: McGraw-Hill), pp. 100–103. Tertullian's acceptance of a Montanist stance shows the extent to which Montanism represented an emphasis upon the active spirit of prophecy which went well beyond Montanus personally.

CHAPTER 8 PARADIGMATIC THINKING IN AUGUSTINE

1 See Chilton and Neusner, (1995) *Judaism in the New Testament. Practices and Beliefs* (London and New York: Routledge).

2 Victor P. Furnish, (1984) *II Corinthians* Anchor Bible 32A (Garden City, Doubleday), p. 330.

3 That is the theme of the brilliant work by Lloyd G. Patterson, (1967) *God and History in Early Christian Thought:* Studies in Patristic Thought (New York: Seabury).

4 Ibid., p. 55.

5 See Walter Rauschenbusch, [from 1917] (1960) *A Theology for the Social Gospel* (New York: Abingdon), and the discussion in Chilton (ed.), (1984) *The Kingdom of God in the Teaching of Jesus:* Issues in Religion and Theology 5 (Philadelphia: Fortress), p. 6.

6 See Eusebius, *The History of the Church* (trans. G. A. Williamson) (1975) (Minneapolis: Augsburg), p. 8, and *History of the Church* 1.1; 10.4

7 Ibid., 10.9.6–9 and Lloyd G Patterson, (1967) *God and History in Early Christian Thought:* Studies in Patristic Thought (New York: Seabury).

8 For a brief discussion of *City of God,* see E. R. Hardy, (1969) 'The City of God,' *A Companion to the Study of St. Augustine* (ed. R. W. Battenhouse) (New York: Oxford University Press) pp. 257–283.

9 See Stanley Romaine Hopper, "The Anti-Manichean Writings," *A Companion,* pp. 148–174.

10 See Lyford Paterson Edwards, (1919) *The Transformation of Early Christianity from an Eschatological to a Socialized Movement* (Menasha, Wisconsin: Banta), p. 17.

11 For a succinct and illuminating account of the most important issues involved, see Bernard Lonergan, *Method in Theology,* (1972) (New York: Herder), pp. 175–234.

INDEX

Abba, one's relationship to God
through Christ 26–27
apostasy, criticism of Galatians by Paul
27
Aqiba, uncleanness of immersion pool
21–3
Augustine, Saint 137; Christianity in
social history of Roman religion and
Hellenistic philosophy 161–65;
interpretation of the Trinity 81–84;
paradigmatic thinking in arguments
from social history 154–67

baptism and prayer: everyone baptized
considered child of Abraham 37;
faith replacing law 28–9, 34–8;
immersion as "death" to sin 42;
installing spirit of God in one's heart
72–74; as a relationship to God
26–8, 30–1,34–7,40–2
Barrett, C. K. 41

Christianity, baptism as a relationship
to God 26–8, 30–1, 34–7, 40–2
Christiansen, Ellen Juhl 37–8
classification and unity of topics in
philosophy of Rabbinic debate 94–9
cleanness and uncleanness: altar
offering and blemished priest 22–3;
clay oven cut into parts 90–1; honey
and honeycombs 3, 5–6; immersion
pool, requisite volume of water
21–3; potential for actuality of
uncleanness in Mishnaic law 3, 6–8

crucifiction and resurrection: identity
of self with death and resurrection of
Christ 28; as God's reconciliation
with the world 70

Damascus Rule, law code of Qumran
Sect 10–11

ethical conduct derived from Greek
philosophy 73–4
Eusebius of Caesarea, Christianity in
social history and friendship with
Constantine 158–61

Genesis Rabbah, paradigmatic thinking
in Midrash of Rabbinic Judaism
139–43
gnosticism: emergence of 114–28;
Pauline letter to Corinthians 1–14
God, relationship with in Pauline
letters 37–46
golden Rule in Mishnaic legal code 4
Grant, Robert M. 44
Greek influences: Irenaeus, gnosticism,
and Christianity 111–48; in Pauline
letters 70–86

Hays, Richard 32–3
Hebrews as a Christian Judaism 39
high priest and King, power and
authority of in Rabbinic debate
92–4
Hillel, House of, uncleanness of honey
and honeycomb 3